Praise for the author

'This is a lurid tale… yet Clarkson
nothing short of fascinating.'
Independent on Sunday on *Bindon*

D0869176

'Utterly compelling.'
Evening Standard on *Hit 'Em Hard*

'There is no doubt that Spot was a nasty piece of work but
in this well-judged biography Clarkson brings him to life…
BRILLIANT.'
Time Out on *Hit 'Em Hard*

'A thrilling glimpse into a hidden world of money, power,
glamour and violence.'
Sun on *Killing Charlie*

'Reveals a fascinating life, albeit savage and ultimately wasted.'
Loaded on *Killer on the Road*

'Bindon emerges from Clarkson's portrait as a true gent, if a
ferociously violent one, with an unsettling sense of humour.'
Daily Telegraph on *Bindon*

'Jack Spot's legend is still frighteningly alive in Wensley Clarkson's hands.'
Sunday Express on *Hit 'Em Hard*

WENSLEY CLARKSON has investigated numerous crimes across the world for the past thirty years. His research has included prison visits, surveillance operations, police raids and even post mortems. Clarkson's books – published in more than thirty countries –have sold more than two million copies. He has made numerous documentaries in the UK, US, Australia and Spain and written TV and movie screenplays. His most recent major TV project is Florida-based drama series *Boca Grande* which he created, developed and wrote with BAFTA award-winning *Peaky Blinders* director David Caffrey. Clarkson's recent book *Sexy Beasts* – about the Hatton Garden raid – was nominated for a Crime Writers' Association Dagger award.

www.wensleyclarkson.com

THE CROSSING

The Shocking Truth About
Gang Wars in Brexit Britain

WENSLEY CLARKSON

JOHN BLAKE

Published by John Blake Publishing,
The Plaza,
535 King's Road,
Chelsea Harbour,
London SW10 0SZ

www.johnblakebooks.com

www.facebook.com/johnblakebooks
twitter.com/jblakebooks

This edition first published in 2019

Paperback ISBN: 978 1 78946 121 3
Ebook ISBN: 978 1 78946 145 9

British Library Cataloguing-in-Publication Data:

A catalogue record for this book is available from the British Library.

Design by www.envydesign.co.uk

Printed and bound in Great Britain by Clays Ltd, Elcograf S.p.A.
1 3 5 7 9 10 8 6 4 2

Papers used by John Blake Publishing are natural, recyclable products made
from wood grown in sustainable forests. The manufacturing processes
conform to the environmental regulations of the country of origin.

Every reasonable effort has been made to trace copyright-holders of
material reproduced in this book, but if any have been inadvertently
overlooked the publishers would be glad to hear from them.

John Blake Publishing is an imprint of Bonnier Books UK
www.bonnierbooks.co.uk

To The Crossing: without it, this story wouldn't exist

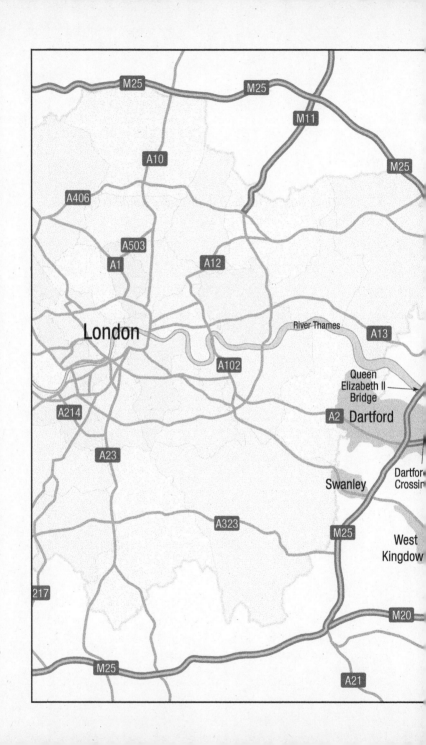

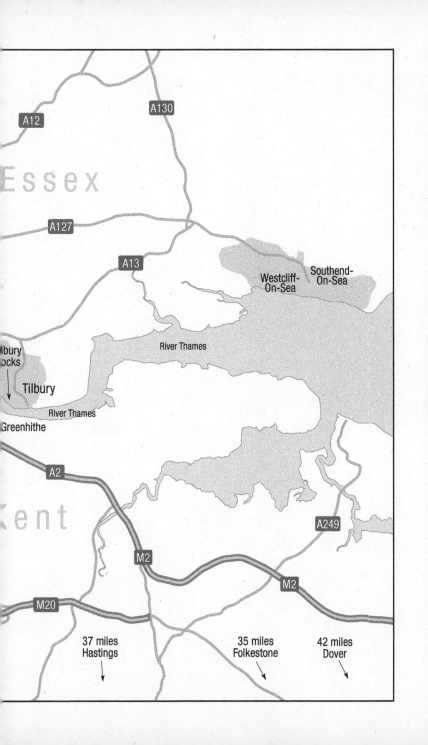

CONTENTS

AUTHOR'S NOTE

The River Thames and the badlands of London, Kent and Essex dominate this story but it is much more than just an exposé of the changing face of UK crime. Many of the criminals I've interviewed down the years had warned me about this new, chilling underworld but I had to see it with my own eyes to completely appreciate how it has evolved.

Within days of starting my research for this book, I realised there were many who didn't want me to expose this new crime phenomenon that now dominates the British underworld. Angry threats to myself and my family, followed by a mystery break-in at my office, felt like warnings. Also, there were some no-shows for meetings in and around the area where The Crossing is located. Clearly, this was a dark and dangerous netherworld few wanted to talk about, but I soldiered on because the key to my investigations inside the UK's crimelands has always been to ignore the threats because if someone really wants to harm myself or my family, they'll just do it, rather than give me an advance warning.

'No one will want to talk to you,' one former policeman in Kent told me just before I agreed to write this book. He turned out to be wrong, but only because I refused to take no for an answer and convinced many of my interviewees that I would not reveal their names.

By a strange twist of fate there was usually a ferocious wind whistling around The Crossing whenever I visited. In the nearby areas of Kent and Essex, so closely associated with professional criminals for many years, I found deserted properties where British gangsters once lived before they were chased off their own homelands by a psychotic new breed of deadly gangster who had targeted this unfriendly corner of Kent, the so-called Garden of England.

At times that same wind screamed so loudly in the areas around The Crossing that it made it doubly hard to hear anyone when I talked to them outside. Then again, many of them clearly didn't want to hear what I was saying in the first place and not even a gale force wind could drown out the verbal abuse I received from those who refused point-blank to help and slammed their doors in my face. Indeed, many who know the characters involved in this story later admitted they were amazed some of them hadn't waved a gun in my face because, as I was about to discover, firearms are prevalent across these badlands.

This story takes place today – now – but the history of the area's underworld going back hundreds of years has played a crucial role in what has evolved, in and around The Crossing.

My undeniable curiosity about The Crossing and all that it represents was first fuelled more than ten years ago. I was investigating the fallout from 1983's world-record-breaking Brink's-Mat gold bullion raid when so-called old school gangsters, who once thrived in that same area, were at their most powerful. Then gun-crazy gangs from abroad began making inroads into these swathes of prime crime territory. One retired Scotland Yard detective told me back then: 'The foreign gangs have started slaughtering the old-time British criminals. They're gonna run this area one day.'

I was stunned that a place so deeply immersed in the history of British crime could be at the centre of such a cold-blooded underworld war right on the doorstep of London. Then, as I began investigating the background to The Crossing, I realised I'd stumbled on one of the UK's most disturbing and chilling crime stories.

Ultimately, this book revolves around a way of life, a tough mentality deeply influenced by all the criminals you are going to read about here. To this day, many believe that none of this would have happened if the UK wasn't so closely connected to Europe and beyond. That's debatable, to say the least. But unpeeling this tale left me with myriad impressions of today's UK underworld and all the characters you are about to meet. As I researched and wrote this book, I realised some of my sources had shady, ulterior motives. My aim has always been to show this story in a balanced light, not a version warped by the evil intent of people on both sides of the divide. Also, I wish to apologise in advance to the law-abiding citizens of every country whose criminals have recently landed on British shores. Of course, the majority of people from these countries deserve our utmost respect. The gangsters you are about to read about represent the tiniest section of these populations and in no way reflect the true character of the people.

In this book I've used the term 'foreigners' many times to describe the criminals who have turned up on UK shores. I'm genuinely not sure if it is an acceptable term in modern-day Britain. It's still used by many in this country but often as part of blanket, discriminatory and negative responses towards people from other countries. My intention is NOT to fuel those fires but to try and explain how and why The Crossing has become the most criminally active area in Britain today. I've even tried to come up with a better word than 'foreigners' but since it's not actually a derogatory term in itself, I decided to stick to using it within these pages and I'm sorry if anyone finds the word offensive.

The story you are about to read may not be the one that most criminals would have preferred to be told, but it is the nearest to the truth about an underworld that has left a mark on everyone it has touched, from the hard-pressed local police force to the families of victims of crime, even the criminals themselves. During the course of my research I've been taken into the confidence of many individuals who, for obvious reasons, would prefer to remain anonymous. I have respected their wishes and need only say that my decision to do so was as much to protect the guilty as the innocent, as well as ensuring the safety of many people in close-knit communities. As a result, some of the scenes depicted here represent a combination of facts reconstructed to reflect events as they were told to me. Certain characterisations, incidents, locations and dialogue were composited for dramatic purposes and to help protect the identity of my sources. This means many of the names have had to be changed. But in writing this book I hope to have dispersed the mystique of a brutal, relentless underworld that has overshadowed everything else in its path.

THE CROSSING

Close to the vast steel girders of The Crossing is a cluster of abandoned car parks, rundown warehouses and a handful of residential blocks of flats. This once-vibrant area links the troubled past of The Crossing with today's real-life criminals, who you're going to read about – it is a tragedy of Shakespearean proportions.

Wensley Clarkson
London, 2019

CAST OF CHARACTERS

Bari – Pint-sized Albanian drug lord from hell

Brian – Fearless old-school underworld legend

Cenki – Gangster with a unique lifestyle

Danny – Brexiteer gangster dreams of a comeback

Darren – Softly-spoken Brit who works for 'the enemy'

Dragon – Slippery boss of The Tunnel Boys

Driza – Albanian serial killer-turned-henchman

Felicia – Gang boss's widow with a vice secret

Frank – Crumbling old-school armed robber

Gorgi – Ukrainian 'ice' merchant

Keith – Loyal villain with a taste for guns

Kill – Psychotic Romanian kingpin

La Patrona (aka Carmela) – Latin America's London-based
 lady boss

Lou – crime vet out to settle the score

Maria – Queen of the Shipping Containers

Misha – Russian mobster with no more friends in high places

Monica and Kandra – Mother-and-daughter contract killers

Paulina – Queen of the Pot Growers

Peta – Coke-cutting king

Ray – Double-dealing woman cop selling guns on the side

Ruk the Collector – Ultimate money man

Sav – Short-fused Romanian crime boss

Teddy – Old-school villain who watched his back

The Dad – Slippery Romanian inspired by the Pink Panther gang

The Ghost – Shadowy UK-based Russian billionaire

The Hanna brothers – British sharks who got caught

The Odessa Boys – Loaded Ukrainian gangsters

The Tunnel Boys – Ruthless Romanian gang

Terry – Veteran blagger

Tinag – Disabled heroin king

Tommy Boy – Scousers' secret weapon

Toni – Half-British/half-Albanian scooter boy boss

Vlad – Russian king of the launderers

Vulo – Moldovan pimp from hell

If a writer knows enough about what he is writing about, he may omit things that he knows. The dignity of movement of an iceberg is due to only one-ninth of it being above water.

Ernest Hemingway

A boat of dirty and disreputable appearance, with two figures in it, floated on the Thames as an autumn evening was closing in. The figures in this boat were those of a strong man with ragged grizzled hair and a sun-browned face, and a dark girl of nineteen or twenty. The girl rowed, pulling a pair of sculls very easily; the man, with the rudder-lines slack in his hands, kept an eager look-out. He had no net, hook or line, and he could not be a fisherman; and he could not be a waterman ... but his eyes watched every little race and eddy. She watched his face as earnestly as he watched the river. But, in the intensity of her look there was a touch of dread or horror.

Charles Dickens, *Our Mutual Friend*

You divide the world into two categories: those who kill and those who don't. You think that because I am a woman I belong to the latter. You're wrong.

Donna Imma, *Gomorrah*

PROLOGUE

Welcome to a strange, deadly *Gommorah*-style shadowy netherworld that revolves around The Dartford Crossing and the badlands of London, Kent and Essex. This book exposes the uncomfortable truth about racism and bigotry in Brexit-tainted Britain today.

And at the centre of it all is the iconic Dartford Crossing that links Kent and Essex – the perfect metaphor for a country that is split down the middle. This truly is a tale of two nations.

The Crossing is all about subtle criminality. The uncomfortable truth is that you can't help admiring the gall and organisational skills of the foreign gangsters who feature in this book as they conquer the UK's most lucrative underworld territories from the ignorant, Brexiteer-type old-school local villains.

One of the biggest ironies of the 2016 EU Referendum is that many British citizens who voted to leave Europe believed the withdrawal of the UK from the European Union would help stamp out the invasion of foreign criminals on UK shores. Nothing could be further from the truth. Since the Brexit vote more foreign criminals than ever have arrived on British soil and few intend leaving, if and when the UK's departure from Europe goes ahead.

Many of the bitter and twisted old-school British gangsters who feature in this book are convinced that once the UK separates itself from Europe the way will be clear for them to return to underworld dominance, especially in the badlands of Kent and Essex close to The Dartford Crossing, which is at the centre of this story.

Former bank robber Billy told me: 'We voted to get out of Europe because we want those foreign bastards to leave our shores and they'll have to fuck off once this all goes through.'

But that simply isn't the case, as you will discover in this book. Indeed, the foreign gangs are thriving and have pushed local gangsters out of the picture almost completely. As one Albanian drug lord told me: 'We don't care about fuckin' Brexit. Britain is richer than most other countries and [it's] easy to make big money here. Nothing will change that. I know British gangsters think that Brexit will help them but they're wrong.'

Eighty-three-year-old Pat was once Kent's busiest drug smuggler until the Eastern Europeans appeared on the scene. He said: 'The old-school British villains need their heads examined. The foreign gangs are ruthless and they'll shoot them all if they have to. I've told my mates to put their shooters away for good and find an honest way to earn a living or retire. Nothing's worth dying for.

'This country is the perfect marketplace for all these foreign gangsters. They can sell their drugs, run their brothels and clean all their dirty cash here. Why would they even contemplate going back to their own shithole countries?'

So here you have it. The UK's new criminal badlands run and dominated by gangs from other countries.

PROLOGUE

As one Romanian gangster put it: 'We're in charge now. The British criminals thought they had the right to run things here. They believed they were entitled to it because they were born in this country. Well, they're not. We are here to stay.'

1

THE RIVER

The first hint of The Crossing came through thick fog as the two imposing towers of the 500-foot-tall Queen Elizabeth II Bridge loomed majestically through the mist like something out of a Disney fairy tale. It was mid-afternoon on 10 March 2013.

This extraordinary half-mile-long structure straddles what they call the 'mouth' of a great river, which leads to one of the most vibrant cities on earth. At least fourteen million people rely on goods transported along the Thames or using The Crossing. In the two underground tunnels of The Crossing that take traffic north into Essex, vehicles drive through a neon-lit hollow subterranean concrete tube under the Thames before emerging into the badlands of an English county that contains more shotgun licences than anywhere else in Britain.

The weather conditions round these parts vary enormously, almost from one hour to the other. Today, with visibility on the bridge down to no more than thirty feet, it was left to good caution as motorists negotiated the four crowded lanes of the carriageway of the Queen Elizabeth II Bridge taking them south into Kent.

That afternoon, the eerie sound of distant fog horns on the Thames was just about heard by drivers as they struggled towards the biggest river crossing in Europe through the thick mist which had slowed most of them down to 20mph. Bitterly cold crosswinds cut in from the estuary below. The links and floating cables of the bridge seemed stretched to breaking point as the enormous structure moved slightly from side to side. With the breeze gradually dispersing the mist, the entire bridge appeared on the horizon as if it was suspended in mid-air.

* * *

Frank Carter, forty-four, was what people in Kent and Essex call an 'old-school gangster', a convicted armed robber. Carter had been to prison and was now struggling to survive back in the real world, despite getting a new job as a used car salesman. The police near his home in Buckinghamshire, west of London, believed that he had committed another robbery since his release. He'd told his family he was innocent and accused the police of harassing him because he had a criminal record. But then that's what most old-school gangsters would say.

Earlier that day, Carter had had an emotional meeting with his ageing mother in nearby Erith, Kent, which had ended abruptly after she refused to lend him any money. As he began the long drive home to Buckinghamshire, he must have felt at the end of his tether.

What was the point in going on? No future. No life. Of course, in some ways, Carter had brought it all on himself. After leaving prison there had been two choices: go back to thieving or go straight. He'd chosen the honest path and got himself a job selling cars but he wasn't very good at it, by all accounts.

It may well have crossed his mind to end his life like so many others when he was locked up in prison. But those thoughts had eventually passed as he counted down the months, weeks and finally days until he was back in the free world. However, the free world hadn't turned out to be any more welcoming than life inside. Times had changed, according to his underworld associates. Gangs of trigger-happy foreign criminals were taking over, there was no room for good old-fashioned British robbers.

Carter had been going steadily downhill since leaving prison. Back home, he'd discovered that many of his family members were deeply embarrassed and ashamed by his criminal record.

As he found himself that afternoon in March 2013 approaching The Crossing – a transport hub he'd used many times during his lifetime – it must have reminded him of how his fellow inmates back in prison had frequently talked about this being the El Dorado of crime in south-east England: the gateway to the UK's most lucrative underworld, or at least it had been for Carter and others before he went to prison.

As he headed towards The Crossing that misty afternoon, Carter called his wife and told her: 'I've had enough. They're never going to leave me alone, I'm going to jump off the bridge.' He then pressed the Off button on his phone and, a few moments later, slammed the brakes on his car, pulled up and jumped out. So immersed in his own hopeless world was he that he completely ignored the many hooting vehicles narrowly avoiding him as they drove past on the busy four-lane carriageway. Behind him, the mid-afternoon traffic heading south towards the bridge began to slow down even more. In the distance, police sirens could soon be clearly heard above the din of the traffic.

Glancing in their rear-view mirrors, motorists spotted three white police SUVs and moved their vehicles obediently to one side to let the motorway patrol cruisers through. Ahead, other motorists ground to a complete halt on the cusp of the steeply angled carriageways that climbed from the north, Essex side of the Queen Elizabeth II Bridge. Ahead of this now-static traffic jam – caused by Carter's decision to stop his car on the bridge – those three police cars slewed across all four lanes of the carriageway, blocking the traffic. Officers emerged from the three cars and headed hurriedly over on foot towards two sets of railings straddling the bicycle lane on the offside of the bridge. To their left, Frank Carter stood by the railings immediately overlooking the river.

Many of those in the traffic jam noticed something was happening and arched to get a better view. Behind them a long line of vehicles began snaking miles back into the heartlands of Essex.

At the side of the bridge, Carter remained, standing precariously close to the edge as those police officers approached. Having found the highest point of the bridge on The Crossing that bitterly cold and gusty afternoon, he was now threatening to end his life on the very structure that had become synonymous with more criminal activity than anywhere else in Britain and Europe combined.

For the next three hours Carter stood and listened to the police officers trying to coax him down. It was so cold up there that he and the officers' voices trembled and their breath had long since turned to steam.

When asked why he'd chosen The Crossing, Carter explained to the police officers that he'd been born in nearby Erith in the heart of what old-school British professional criminals to this day still call 'sawn-off shotgun territory' because of the number of armed robbers coming from that area.

Almost apologetically, Carter even explained to the officers that was why the police had always been his sworn enemy. In a shaky voice he informed them that he believed the police near his new home in Buckinghamshire on the west side of London had been watching him for weeks because he was suspected of taking part in another robbery since his release from prison.

Ironically, the very same police who had made him so paranoid in the first place now stood between Frank Carter and certain death. Carter even managed a slight smile as he pointed this out to the officers. He then tried to look directly into all their eyes to see if they really cared.

To most of the policemen and women there that day, Carter must have been just another sad, lonely, desperate figure who they had a duty to try and save. As time passed, Carter began to struggle to find any more words to say to them and started making more calls on his mobile to his family and friends. Each conversation ended abruptly. Behind him and those police officers an even longer stream of traffic had built up and was now stretching back many miles into Essex, past the nearby Lakeside Shopping Centre where so many of the gangsters Carter knew took their families at weekends.

Many of these characters from South London, Kent and Essex ran the underworld in this part of the country for many years. Their names were indelibly stamped on the conscience of this area but now they were having to make way for a new, more chilling type of criminal, making his blood-thirsty mark on the badlands of England. No wonder Carter felt like yesterday's man as he stood there on the edge of The Crossing.

Hundreds of feet below him, a small tanker steamed slowly through the dispersing fog on its way up Old Father Thames towards London. Just west of The Crossing, a police boat left its mooring and headed past the tanker in the opposite direction, having been alerted to the Carter 'problem'.

The vast river below Frank Carter's feet wasn't much changed since the days when Charles Dickens' gritty fictional characters struggled for survival on its banks, but the shoreline itself was altered beyond recognition, especially since the Queen Elizabeth II Bridge – part of The Crossing system – had been opened by Her Majesty back in 1991.

Little did she know that The Crossing would evolve into a pivotal gateway for the UK underworld. By linking Kent and Essex, it provided gangsterdom with a wide-open marketplace in the richest corner of England. As one old-school British criminal put it later: 'When the Queen, bless her, opened that bridge, we was happy as pie because we knew it would make our jobs simpler. Robbing banks and security vans, smuggling loads of drugs for huge, fat profits. The Crossing made it all easier.'

Back on the bridge, that chilly day in March 2013, Frank Carter moved slightly closer to the edge and glanced down at the water rippling hundreds of feet beneath him. He looked across at the officers again and began swearing at them angrily – particularly one specialist detective who had just arrived to lead the negotiations.

Carter made yet another phone call. This time he cried as he spoke to someone. Then he ended the call, turned towards the police officers and started swearing again.

The specialist detective later recalled that the 'horrible' weather conditions made the situation even worse: 'It was the coldest place I've ever been in my life,' he explained.

Every now and then, Carter threatened to jump. The officers feared with the ever-increasing crosswinds, he might accidentally fall.

Any rapport the police officers had achieved earlier with Carter was now gone. Between yet more phone calls he was shouting erratically. Then, suddenly, Carter softened his attitude and tried to shake the specialist detective's hand – but it wasn't in a gesture of friendship or trust. As that detective later recalled: 'It was as if he wanted permission to jump, which I wasn't going to do.'

Finally, officers managed to coax Carter towards them with the offer of a good old-fashioned British cup of tea. They then grabbed him, but he struggled and fought back furiously. The specialist detective explained: 'We held onto him for as long as we could. He fought – he didn't want to be grabbed. We used all our strength.'

Despite the efforts of three officers, Carter managed to free himself from their grip and darted back to the railings on the edge of the bridge.

The officers stared at each other in horror.

No doubt part of Frank Carter's life must have flashed before his eyes as he stood there, thinking through his next move. Below him, approaching the bridge from the west side, was that police boat, chugging steadily east towards them. Carter glanced down and watched it for a few moments – they all knew why it was on its way.

The police officers said no more. In some ways it was a subliminal sign of respect and acceptance: they had done everything in their power to stop him, whatever was about to happen now was beyond their control.

In complete silence, Carter looked up at the cloudy sky and leaned closer towards the edge of the railings. Casually and silently, he flipped over the bannister and out into the thin air, disappearing from sight.

Frank Carter fell hundreds of feet so fast that he stood no chance of surviving.

The police at the railings above could barely hear the plop as his body hit the water.

* * *

Within a couple of minutes, the same police boat Carter had been watching only a short while earlier moved alongside his broken, lifeless body and hauled it on board. Later, he was pronounced dead at nearby Darent Valley Hospital although the officers on the boat that afternoon knew full well he was gone the moment they saw his body smash into the water.

The death of Frank Carter sums up the power and influence of The Crossing. It is undoubtedly an awe-inspiring piece of architectural engineering. Ultimately, the thousands of vehicles waiting in that traffic jam were more concerned about their journeys being delayed than the life and crimes of a sad ex-bank robber who'd decided to end it all in such dramatic fashion. But the fact that the convicted criminal chose The Crossing as the place where he would die is significant when you consider its close association with Britain's ever-changing underworld.

Carter – a bank robber from the classic old school of British professional criminals – had struggled when pitted against the new, sharp, superbly organised foreign gangsters now turning The Crossing into the UK's gateway to billions of pounds worth of crime.

* * *

Millions of years ago the Thames flowed north-east from the exact point where The Crossing now stands. At the end of the last Ice Age enormous quantities of meltwater forged through the river, cutting through the overlooking chalky hills to create a new south-easterly course for the river that exists to this day.

The Thames itself was then used as a border until at least as late as the tenth century. Coins found north and south of the river close to The Crossing were made by two different tribes, the Catuvellauni and Atrebates. As the river bank became the scene of numerous blood-thirsty clashes between the four-teenth and seventeenth centuries, many were slain.

It is also believed that somewhere deep beneath the river-bed close to The Crossing lies the wreck of a small galleon packed with stolen gold, buried so deep in a mudbank that no one has ever managed to find it, even at the lowest of low tides.

'There's something about this place that reeks of crime,' one local criminologist told me. 'Everywhere you look, there is evidence of it. It's surreal yet inviting. Those criminals in that galleon must have been so desperate to be prepared to risk their lives on such a venture.'

So, thousands of bodies are buried close to where The Crossing stands today. Burial mounds and barrows were used for the ceremonies as part of a special ritual for the dead. The spirits of these corpses haunt the banks of the river close to where this story is centred. Some even claim that the ghosts of victims can be heard screaming out across the water, especially on misty, moonless nights.

Charles Dickens' influence on this part of the world is undeniable. He was the first person to publicly expose the criminal badlands that dominated the banks of the Thames during Victorian times, even as far east as Dartford. Dickens' own horror and fear of the river was embedded in what he'd witnessed first hand. His vivid opening scene in *Our Mutual Friend* refers to a man who makes his living fishing dead bodies out of the Thames.

The corpses in Dickens' book represent a thousand secrets and the same might be said today of any of the corpses frequently washed ashore near The Crossing. And Dickens' vivid description of young women being taken across the river to work in the brothels and workhouses of East London accurately reflects some of the modern stories you will read here.

Today, the Thames may well be much quieter and more peaceful in some of its more rural settings, but the river's estuary close to The Crossing is exactly the opposite. Only as recently as the Second World War, soldiers patrolled the riverbanks as fears of an invasion by Adolf Hitler reached their peak in the twelve months following the outbreak of war in 1939.

Many of these historical conflicts mirror the clashes that occurred between the old-school criminals of Kent and Essex as recently as the 1990s. These modern-day highwaymen saw themselves as guardians of their respective territories and mortal enemies.

Ironically, it would be the influx of foreign criminals over even more recent times that would force two criminal 'tribes' from Essex and Kent to join forces in an attempt to see off these so-called invaders. But the pressure on these old-fashioned British gangsters often proved too much for even them to handle.

* * *

At least 200,000 containers pass beneath, above or over The Crossing every year at exactly the point where Frank Carter's body hit the water that day in March 2013. You can be certain many of those containers hold illegal goods. From stolen cars to drugs to people, they will have seen it all – if they could talk, they'd reveal a myriad of secrets.

'Containers are a beautiful thing for a criminal,' explained old-time Kent gangster Larry Tindall. 'You can put anything you want inside them and, if they're sealed, the chances are no one will bother to look to see what they contain.'

Shipping containers are called *enë të anijeve* in Albanian and a variety of unpronounceable words in other languages, but all the criminals operating in and around The Crossing know them as simply 'containers' even if they don't speak any other words of English. You see, containers are the lifeblood of this story. When they were first invented just after the end of World War Two, few would have guessed that they could have single-handedly been responsible for so many crime waves across the globe, from the crooked port at Naples to the illicit contents of the enormous container ships gliding into Hong

Kong Harbour. So it's no surprise that the development of shipping containers as the world's main mode of transport for all goods neatly parallels the story of how Kent, Essex and London evolved into the vicious ganglands of today.

The year 1956 is when shipping containers were officially launched across the commercial world. It also happens to have been the year when many of the area's most notorious bank robbers and professional criminals first started making a name for themselves. Both were to have a far-reaching effects on the UK underworld. Indeed, containers were invented to help prevent the theft of items in transit across the world's oceans in the first place. But ironically they then became the criminals' favourite mode of transport because they were so easy to hide things in, thanks to their size and being sealed before they are transported.

Shipping containers certainly played a pivotal role in transforming the River Thames, both east and west of The Crossing. Undoubtedly, they helped encourage the modernisation of nearby Tilbury Docks, so that it could accommodate some of the globe's largest container ships. But the story of the connections between the development of shipping containers and the development of the most successful band of criminals ever known in the UK opens up even further in the 1970s. That was when containers became the most used form of transporting goods the world had ever seen and those same gangs of outlaws virtually ruled the streets of London, robbing and stealing from banks and security vans with impunity. But then the story of shipping containers and the UK's professional criminals starts to go in different directions. Today, 90 per cent of the world's goods are transported in containers but those once phenomenally successful gangs of Kent and Essex criminals are now just a faded memory. Their locally born and bred replacements never managed to replicate the success of their predecessors, which then opened up a void in the British underworld thus enabling gangsters from across the globe, especially Eastern Europe, to flood into Britain via The Crossing.

Today's so-called state-of-the-art shipping containers are meant to all be fitted with remote tracking systems so that companies can track their goods, but this has done nothing to stop the use of containers by criminals across the world. In fact, many believe today's shipping containers have helped foreign criminals to dominate the British underworld because they have provided perfect transportation facilities to smuggle everything from drugs to black money.

* * *

These days, shipping containers are taken off the ships at Tilbury by vast prehistoric-looking cranes, then neatly stacked one on top of the other to await transportation to their final destinations. Tilbury – six miles by river from The Crossing – remains the largest port on the Thames and has its own deep-water facilities, specially designed to aid the huge container ships that can only sail this far upriver.

Many of these vessels are bigger than Piccadilly Circus and Leicester Square combined. A lot of them come from China, often via other destinations where illegal goods can be easily added to the load. The skippers of these sea-faring monsters are masters at negotiating the relatively small River Thames and its ferocious currents and erratic tides.

Most of these shipping containers are eventually put on the back of lorries or transported by train from the nearby Tilbury Loop line. Tilbury is also Europe's largest terminal for refrigerated containers and therein lies the key to why the area around it – including The Crossing – is today of such great value to criminals.

Inside those vast, sealed ice boxes all sorts of contraband can be stored without fear that it will be damaged by heat or water during its long and sometimes perilous journey across the oceans. Also, there are the containers that travel away from the UK in the opposite direction, either on ships or the back of lorries. Often they hold items stolen from inside Britain. Meanwhile, the motorway carriageway over The Crossing itself provides a speedy getaway for foreign criminals heading home to Eastern Europe and beyond.

These days, Tilbury is also the main entry point for ships from Rotterdam and Antwerp, which are renowned for containing drugs and stolen gold. From Tilbury, smaller vessels head further upriver to deliver their goods into the heart of London. As a result, the land between The Crossing and Tilbury has long been significant for criminals operating in these parts. This may be part of the reason why The Crossing itself has evolved into, in many ways, a law unto itself. Its tentacles reach across almost every aspect of life in the darkest corners of Kent and Essex, as well as much of London.

* * *

Today, the UK is said to be still in the midst of a boom time when it comes to drugs. But most British criminals and their old-time enemy the police have no doubt this has been further fuelled by foreign gangs turning up on those shores in their droves.

Home Office statistics released in March 2019 showed the amount of drugs seized by UK Border Force and police officers surged by almost a third in 2018, with officials seizing 5,516 kilos – the highest quantity since 2003. It's believed that more than 80 per cent of those drugs have been handled by foreign gangsters based in the UK and most of them are undoubtedly regular users of The Crossing.

* * *

So, it is the Queen Elizabeth II Bridge which casts the biggest shadow over the areas surrounding The Crossing. The sheer size of it dominates the skyline for at least ten miles in all directions. It's impossible to drive around these parts without seeing that bridge looming in the distance.

The River Thames was once the key dominant force in this area. After all, one wouldn't exist without the other. But the river itself has in a sense become something of a diversion. Today, it's the land – the real estate – which drives forward this strange, inhospitable netherworld.

The embankment of both sides of the river overlooked by The Crossing provides an essential barrier between the water and the high-rise tower blocks, industrial estates, empty warehouses, petrol stations, sprawling deserted lorry parks and tatty corner shops dominating this rundown neighbourhood.

Many people who live in the shadow of The Crossing give little or no thought to the river these days. Instead, their lives revolve around the secretive criminal habitat which has emerged in recent years to become part of the fabric of this community.

In nearby Greenhithe – a working-class area overlooked by The Crossing's majestic Queen Elizabeth II Bridge – water-blown corpses occasionally wash up on the shoreline near to where council estate kids play on vast swathes of barren wasteland.

One resident explained: 'When the currents are strong, all the old shit that's been dropped in the water around The Crossing area ends up washing up near us. I've found three bodies there over the past few years. Not a pretty sight, I can tell you that!'

As dawn breaks on the shore at Greenhithe and its close neighbour Dartford, The Crossing resembles a vast, eerily back-lit Meccano toy set, with pinprick-sized cars and trucks gliding across the distant bridge. Locals say that on most spring mornings, the sound of truck gearboxes grinding noisily in the distance cuts right through the dawn chorus.

'That fuckin' bridge looks down on us like some kind of creature from hell!' said one home owner living within a stone's throw of The Crossing. 'We hate it because it's turned this area inside out. There's no heart and soul here anymore – just a procession of lorries, often with massive containers circling the area, crunching their gearboxes and up to no good.'

The small side roads and B-routes of this very same rundown industrial and residential area start right under the shadow of the massive girders of the Queen Elizabeth II Bridge and play a significant role in this story. Few people ever venture out onto these streets, especially after darkness falls. Many of those living in the immediate vicinity acknowledge that bad things are happening within a stone's throw of wherever they live or work (or both). Locals also claim the police rarely venture out into these parts.

As night-time falls, this area grows silent and edgy, filled with shadows accompanied by the distant omnipresent sound of motor vehicles surging south over the bridge and north through the tunnel of The Crossing.

* * *

Going back at least fifty years, most shipping containers destined for London were handled by dockers working on the doorstep of the city at the East India docks and Canary Wharf close to the financial community. Many of these dockers were the fathers of some of the most notorious criminals ever to emerge from the streets of postwar London. And some of those poorly paid fathers used their jobs as dockers to help 'train up' their sons by showing a complete disregard for honesty, something they always blamed on the poverty-stricken state of London following the end of World War II.

'Dockers back in them days often supplemented their income by stealing stuff from the ships and then selling it in the local pubs later that same evening,' explained old-time British bank robber Davy, whose father was one such docker.

'Everyone did it, back in them days. War rationing was still in place and you had to beg, steal or borrow to feed yer family.

'My old man had no choice but to steal to keep us all properly fed. I watched him dissolve into drink and anger most nights because he was under so much pressure to provide for us all – we all suffered as a result. So, I pledged to meself that I'd go out there and pull off bank heists and security van stick-ups because I didn't wanna struggle like him.'

So that's how the Thameside communities of South London, Kent and Essex became such fertile breeding grounds for postwar criminals, who had spent much of their childhoods using bombsites as playgrounds. Those very same characters helped turn this region into the criminal badlands of Britain by the time the Swinging Sixties were underway. But then this was the so-called golden age of UK crime when professional criminals ruled the streets of London.

Before The Crossing ever existed, dozens of small boats struggled back and forth across this often-choppy stretch of the Thames each day. A combination of strong tides, vicious currents and the backwash from larger vessels made the journey extremely hazardous.

Frank explained: 'This area was far enough from London for people to think they could get away with stuff they wouldn't do in the city. Trouble is, it turned this area into a den of fuckin' thieves.'

Back in postwar times, this same stretch of the river saw at least one person a day drowned and most of those victims were either fully fledged criminals or working for villains, who used the boats to transport stolen goods.

Dartford – and all the other communities close to The Crossing – has never managed to shake off the connection with crime.

'People in the rest of Kent look down on this area as a place where bad things happen,' says Frank.

* * *

Until the completion of The Crossing less than thirty years ago, the most popular way to travel between Kent and Essex was through leaky Victorian-built tunnels running beneath the River Thames close to Central London. In the mid-1970s, one daring band of security van robbers had the audacity to hold up a cash-in-transit vehicle in the middle of one of those tunnels. This outrageous, headline-hitting heist sparked a deadly war between the big gangs of professional London criminals and Scotland Yard's Flying Squad, who were rumoured to have introduced an unofficial shoot-to-kill policy when it came to stopping robbers in their tracks.

A number of what were alleged to be unnecessary shootings of criminals by detectives caused real and vicious hatred between the robbers and the 'cozzers', as the police were known to many in those days. Then – just a few years after that deadly era came to a close – some highly lucrative robberies occurred. These included the largest bullion heist in criminal history at a Brink's-Mat warehouse near Heathrow Airport, in November 1983. Raiders got away with almost £30 million worth of gold that would fetch upwards of half a billion pounds on the gold market today.

Old-school British criminal Rob explained: 'The police virtually gave up after we pulled off the Brink's-Mat job and a couple of other really big robberies. We was running rings round 'em – it was a good time for villains back then.'

Towards the mid-1980s, some of those so-called big-name London gangsters decided to kick back and enjoy the fruits of their crimes, heading for sunnier climes on southern Spain's notorious Costa del Crime, where there was no extradition treaty between Spain and the UK at the time. Around this time, robbery became a much more risky enterprise and far less lucrative, thanks to a proliferation of CCTV, credit cards and wages being paid directly into bank accounts.

'Some of the British lads then got involved in drug smuggling because "going across the pavement" – as we all called robbery back then – was getting riskier and the rewards were not so big anymore,' said Rob.

Over in the warmer temperatures of the Mediterranean, the British 'faces' sometimes came across gangsters from as far afield as Eastern Europe and South America for the first time. They hated each other on first sight, it seemed.

Rob explained: 'We didn't go near most of the foreigners back then, but I remember some of them were fascinated by the UK. We soon put them right on that – we "owned" our country and no foreign bastard was going to nick it from us!'

Today, many British crime vets concede that drugs were 'the beginning of the end' for many of them. 'Sure, drugs were easy to make big money out of, but pulling off a drug deal usually meant having to deal with those foreign gangsters and a lot of us didn't trust them an inch,' Rob recalled.

Back home in the UK, the old-school gangsters of Kent and Essex still retained large areas of these counties as their own specific territories where drugs brought in from Spain and South America could be distributed. Essex gangster Jess explained: 'We had our territories and no one would overlap into someone's else's – that's the way it was. We never once considered that outsiders might be after our business. We was locals, we ran things – end of story!'

Then came two specific criminal 'events' which shook the professional gangsters of Kent, Essex and London to the core. In 1990, former Great Train robber Charlie Wilson, originally from South London, was gunned down by a young assassin at his hacienda near Marbella after falling out with a South American drug cartel led by the notorious Pablo Escobar, the original 'Narco'.

A couple of years later, three Essex gangsters in their Range Rover were gunned down in cold blood in a quiet lane on the edge of a field, just a few miles north of The Crossing.

'The underworld wobbled with fear,' recalled bank robber Teddy Taylor. 'This was considered steppin' across the line when it came to brutality. Those three dead villains had certainly been asking for it, but no one expected such a chilling response.

'I remember one old boy I'd worked with for thirty years said that the murders were the last straw. Some people started saying they were the work of foreign criminals, who then hot-footed it over The Crossing and back to Eastern Europe. But there weren't many of them around, back in them days, so we took that one with a pinch of salt.

'Some old-school villains from round here took off for places like Spain and Thailand when it became clear those three villains had been deliberately targeted and everyone feared other killings would follow.'

A spate of violent deaths of British gangsters then occurred, including the contract killing of a London drugs baron in Amsterdam.

'The old school criminals were gettin' battered,' Teddy Taylor recalled. 'That's when it first dawned on me that The Crossing had made access to this part of the world much easier. Sure, we were enjoying the freedom of Kent, Essex and London, thanks to it, but so was everyone else who decided to set up shop here.'

Romanian criminal Kill explained: 'We kept hearing that the UK was the best marketplace of all when it came to drugs. Eventually, in the late-nineties, a lot of us started thinking seriously about moving to Britain. The war in Kosovo was over, for the first time in our lives we had a chance to start afresh in a country where money ruled.'

Then in November 2000 came an audacious attempt to steal diamonds worth hundreds of millions of pounds from London's Millennium Dome on the banks of the River Thames, near Greenwich, South-East London. It was eventually foiled by police who had been tipped off by an informant.

'The Millennium Dome job had a far-reaching effect on many old-school British gangsters,' explained bank robber Danny. 'It was a fuckin' disaster. My old man said it was the first time a really big heist had gone completely pear-shaped.'

Some later claimed that if the Millennium Dome gang had consisted of only foreign criminals, they would probably have got away with it because the police would not have been able to infiltrate the gang so easily and foil the raid before it was carried out. But then along came the 9/11 terror attacks in the US and all the usual 'rules of the underworld' were suddenly thrown out of the window. Criminal gangs across the Western world found themselves being more closely monitored than ever before in case they had links to terrorism.

Romanian crime lord Kill explained: 'Moving between countries became much more difficult after 9/11. Most of us stayed in our own territories and tried to work with gangs in other countries when it came to dealing drugs and other things.'

And in Britain and on Spain's Costa del Crime, once-feared and notorious UK criminals were being thrown in prison or taken out by contract killers as their short-lived drug empires began to crumble.

Former robber Rob recalled: 'Drugs made it all more dangerous. Some of the British lads were being culled like animals, especially out in Spain where it was virtually lawless.

'The Spanish cops didn't care if one villain killed another one and it was always about drugs. Some of us started to wonder if we should ease off, take an early retirement and live a bit longer.'

Gangs as far afield as Eastern Europe put their 'expansion plans' on ice because of the 9/11 crackdown. But they still had their eyes and ears to the ground and they knew that the UK had the potential to be their most lucrative marketplace of all in the long term.

Most criminals say that it took four or five years for the law enforcement response sparked by 9/11 to begin to ease. Also, many old-school professional British criminals were struggling with new technology. Some went into semi-retirement because they couldn't cope with computers.

'We came from an era where phone boxes existed and no one knew what the bleedin' internet even meant,' explained one-time bank robber Ned.

So the legendary old dinosaurs were gradually replaced by younger, more erratic English gangs, many of whom did not fully appreciate that foreign criminals had been 'eyeing up' Kent, Essex and London in particular until 9/11 struck.

As Kill explained: 'We waited a few years until all the 9/11 stuff died down, then it was time to make a move.'

* * *

The short but bloody war in Kosova between 1998 and 1999 when ethnic Albanians opposed ethnic Serbs and the government of Yugoslavia undoubtedly helped spark the Albanians' interest in the UK in the first place.

'That's when Albanians began looking for opportunities elsewhere,' explained Albanian drug lord Bari, who has operated as a criminal in the UK for some considerable time. 'We wanted to make big money, but we needed to pick [the] right moment.'

Many Albanians began this process by pretending to be Kosovans fleeing the backlash from the Kosovo War. Criminals from other Eastern European countries would soon follow suit.

The notorious Russian Mafia – mainly from President Vladimir Putin's former home town of St Petersburg – had attached themselves to a number of billionaire oligarchs, who arrived in London just after 9/11.

'The Russian criminals are the most evil and richest of them all. You cross them at your peril,' one UK crime analyst explained.

'The Russian Mafia actively encouraged the Eastern European gangs to make a move into British territory because it was the perfect diversion for them in a sense. The Russians were concentrating on high-end money laundering and even set up a London-based clan especially to clean money for many of Vladimir Putin's mega-rich cronies, who'd come out of communism immensely wealthy. The Eastern Europeans were left to focus on the UK's street-level crime, from drugs to brothels. It was like a pincer movement in a sense and it was brilliantly executed.

'Drugs [are] still [the] biggest money of all today. But fifteen or more years ago, there were still many Eastern Europeans who believed big robberies [were] worth committing, even though British criminals stopped doing them after the Millennium Dome heist went wrong.'

Then, in 2006, three Albanian gangsters who had recently showed up near The Crossing persuaded a group of Kent criminals to join them to carry out potentially the biggest-ever cash robbery in British criminal history.

The Eastern Europeans and the local old-school villains were clearly reluctant partners in the heist, but the Eastern Europeans had planted one of their men 'undercover' in a vast Securitas cash-deposit warehouse on the outskirts of the Kent town of Tonbridge, which they intended to rob. As a result, the Eastern Europeans very much ran the gang. They had only recruited the local criminals because they believed it was vital to keep the British underworld happy if they were to successfully pull off this daring heist.

'I was stunned when I heard that the British lads had agreed to join forces with the foreign villains on that Tonbridge job, but there was a lot of money at stake,' explained now-retired bank robber Paul, from South London, who knew one of the robbers.

The gang's Albanian boss already knew from his inside man that at certain times of the week there was upwards of £50 million in cash inside the depository.

'That's a lot of money in anyone's language,' said Paul. 'But I heard later that the local boys weren't happy from the start with some of the Albanians.'

According to underworld insiders, the British criminals recruited for the Tonbridge gang were told by the Albanians that guns would only be used as a threat on the staff at the depository. It later turned out that two of the Albanian robbers had fought in the Balkans in the late-1990s: 'They were as hard as nails and I think the British boys were a little scared right from the start,' added Paul.

The Crossing played a pivotal role in the Tonbridge heist because of its close proximity to a warehouse owned by the Albanian robbery gang members, where the raiders assembled to plan the job.

'It was only then they started to suspect the Albanians had plans to move into the area near The Crossing on a full-time basis,' explained Paul.

Then the Albanians outlined the robbery plan and the British criminals present got a big shock.

Paul told me: 'The Albanians intended to kidnap the manager of the depot and get alongside his family and threaten to kill them to get him to cooperate.

'The British lads on that job were stunned. The Albanians called it a "Tiger Kidnap". The Brits called it sheer madness, which might end up with someone dying and them getting even longer prison sentences if they was ever caught. The Brits threatened to walk off the job when the Albanians mentioned kidnapping, but in the end they just did as they was told, although they was not happy about it.'

The Tonbridge robbery went ahead on 21 February 2006 and the gang managed to steal more than £50 million after kidnapping Securitas depot manager Colin Dixon and forcing him to provide key codes to the warehouse.

This type of cooperation between foreign and UK criminals should have helped improve the working relationship between the two rival criminal groups: 'But the opposite was true,' explained old-school robber Teddy.

'The Brits and the Albanians turned on each other after the heist because the Brits believed the Albanians had stolen some of the cash for themselves instead of sharing it all out equally after the job as they'd previously agreed.

'The Tonbridge job marked the beginning of the end for those sort of "joint operations". What little trust had existed between us all went completely out of the window.'

Most of the robbers were eventually arrested and imprisoned, although very little of the stolen cash was ever recovered. The chilling fallout from that robbery still sends shivers down the spine of many older Kent and Essex villains to this day.

One British member of the Securitas gang disappeared soon after the raid and was presumed dead. Another gangster connected to the robbery was murdered by a hitman on the Costa del Sol. And another homegrown criminal linked to the heist was almost killed in a hit-and-run attempt outside a Kent pub, which was a notorious underworld haunt. Then a fourth man connected to the Securitas heist killed himself after threats made to his family by Albanian gangsters.

Ex-robber Billy explained: 'The Albanians financed the Securitas robbery and then accused the Brit robbers of grassing their men up to the police. That's the other reason why this all kicked off. The Albanians told the Brits they'd be "running" Kent and Essex and most of London by the end of that decade. And they meant it.'

Ex-bank robber Paul recalled: 'That Tonbridge job was a lesson to all us Brits: never trust the foreign gangs. Never join forces with them, however desperate you might be.'

So, while the Tonbridge gang fell out in spectacular style, other Eastern European criminals recognised that a vacuum was opening up, especially in those areas of Kent and Essex near The Crossing.

'The Albanians who organised the Tonbridge job had warned the Brits in their team that they'd help other Eastern Europeans take everything over if they all fell out and that's exactly what happened,' explained one-time bank robber Teddy.

And there was another unlikely spin-off from the Tonbridge job, too. Following its success, Eastern European gangs targeted other lucrative robbery locations in the UK. They would be the modern equivalent of 1960s bank heists, which so many old school British gangs had once been famous for.

The new foreign gangsters – who'd just arrived in the UK – recognised that old-fashioned traditional banks no longer held large amounts of notes so they focused on cash depots just as they had done during the Tonbridge job which 'earned' them £50 million in cash.

* * *

So, the Eastern European gangsters led by the Albanian Mafia decided it was time to push on into the UK, especially in and around Kent and Essex on either side of The Crossing.

'This area [was] key to running all our stuff in UK. If we controlled The Crossing, then we couldn't fail,' explained Albanian drug lord Bari.

Then the Romanian Mafia – encouraged by other Eastern Europeans gangs – made a direct approach to the Colombian cocaine cartels because they wanted to flood Britain with the drug. Within weeks, they'd agreed a deal with the South Americans to distribute and sell their cocaine on the streets of Britain and the rest of Europe.

Meanwhile, back in Albania, plans were already in place for the country's production of hash in the mountains near Tirana to be tripled in order to provide enough cannabis to supply the whole of the British Isles.

Many of this new wave of Eastern European gangsters did not speak any English, which made the old-school British gangs even more dismissive towards them. One former Kent robber-turned-drug baron called Lonnie explained: 'We couldn't see how they could do anything to us if they couldn't even speak fuckin' English.

'We just wasn't that bothered by what we thought was a small bunch of foreigners. They were just wannabes as far as most of us were concerned. We thought we'd see 'em off easy.'

But behind closed doors, the Albanians and other Eastern European crime clans had secretly agreed to join forces to ensure that no British gang would ever be strong enough to prevent them taking over this lucrative marketplace.

The foreign gangs recognised that for them a key territory was an area near The Crossing between the towns of Dartford, Swanley and West Kingsdown in Kent, three separate communities that had been overrun with criminals for more than fifty years. It was even known to locals as 'The Bermuda Triangle' because, as one resident put it, 'What goes in there doesn't usually come out.'

Murders, big-time bank robberies and massive drugs deals all dominated the Triangle in the recent past, thanks to the many professional criminals who had lived in these three communities down the years.

'This was an area you enter at your peril, or certainly this was the case when the robbers who ruled the London under-world from the sixties to the eighties lived in isolated mansions in the middle of the Bermuda Triangle,' explained old-school bank robber Teddy Taylor.

Taylor had been brought up in a house overlooking the Thames Estuary at Dartford. He recalled: 'My old man would look out of our garden at the tunnel as it was back when there was no bridge and say, "Son, that's where all the duckin' and divin' happens. You need to remember that."

'The Bermuda Triangle is like nowhere else in modern-day Britain. It relies on its own under the radar criminal economy run by villains in the community. It thrives on crime and, as a result, it's been home to some of the area's most powerful gangsters.'

So, foreign gangs targeted the Bermuda Triangle in the belief it would enable them to gain a foothold so they could push on to the most important territories of Kent and Essex and beyond.

The deadly badlands of south-east England were about implode.

2
WAR

In the police control tower overlooking the southern exit from The Crossing, officers noticed a 'red flag' on a black BMW Coupé travelling south at high speed across the Queen Elizabeth II Bridge. It was 7 January 2007.

The police immediately relayed the registration number to their colleagues at security service MI5's headquarters twenty miles further up the Thames, next to the iconic Vauxhall Bridge.

'No action. Repeat, no action,' came the response message from MI5 operatives.

Meanwhile, The Crossing police continued watching the BMW on a small screen as it weaved maniacally in and out of the heavy traffic heading down the four-lane carriageway towards the Channel ports – the gateway to Europe. Less than eleven hours later, the same BMW was about to join a quiet, early-morning motorway intersection near Nice, in Southern France.

As the BMW moved across into the slow lane, a large cement mixer appeared at speed right alongside it, forcing the car to remain in the feeder lane. The truck eventually slowed down enough for the BMW to move over onto the main carriageway, but seconds later, the same cement mixer increased its speed again and was soon just a couple of metres behind the BMW as both sped south on the motorway. Eventually, the cement truck moved out into the middle lane to pass the BMW.

Moments later, the cement mixer pulled right across the lanes and smashed into the side of the BMW with such force that the car was pushed onto the hard shoulder. The cement mixer continued on its journey as if nothing had happened while the now out-of-control BMW smashed over the barrier at the side of the motorway before its nose dipped down towards a ravine, which it bounced towards before exploding into flames.

In London and St Petersburg, news of the crash soon reached the underworld and both country's security services. A man called Misha had been driving the BMW and he'd just fallen out with a London oligarch. Misha had been a member of the Russian St Petersburg Mafia and had known President Vladimir Putin since childhood. At the time, this particular London oligarch was one of Putin's staunchest allies. Putin, it is alleged, had decided his much-rumoured gangster connections needed to be 'cut' so that he could present himself to his beloved Russian public as a clean politician for the next round of elections.

Many believe that the oligarch in question organised the hit as a favour to Putin. But it didn't help him in the long term because the oligarch himself later died in mysterious circumstances after falling out with Putin himself.

It seems the oligarch's paymasters in Moscow wanted him to show them his loyalty by organising the murder of Misha. His death – orchestrated entirely by Russian criminals based in the

UK – was a definite turning point as it showed that foreign criminals in Britain were capable of doing anything they wanted.

'It was a message from Putin and his cronies,' explained former Russian mobster Vlad. 'He was saying, "I can get you anywhere, any time."'

If the police and UK security services had chosen to stop Misha in his BMW that day, perhaps he would never have died. But as one old-school British gangster said: 'Who cares? They'd have got him in the end – they always do.'

Vlad knows the inside story of Misha's fate because he worked alongside him in the St Petersburg Mafia for many years before they both moved to London just after 9/11. The pair's main 'business' was money laundering for oligarchs who had set up home in the UK, as well as for mega-rich criminals back home in Russia.

Vlad later explained: 'Money laundering makes more cash than any other criminal enterprise. The people who do it – like me – are not interested in any other criminal activities. We don't deal in drugs or people, we deal in money, full stop.'

Some have blamed successive British governments for this influx of so-called 'top-end' criminals after Russian oligarchs were offered tempting tax breaks by Tony Blair's New Labour government in the misplaced belief they were legitimate 'businessmen'.

'I don't think the British government realised how many of those oligarchs were themselves criminally involved,' explained Vlad. 'Many of them were "bag carriers" in the days when communism crumbled and helped delivered black money to and from politicians like Yeltsin and Putin.'

But the ease with which the Russian Mafia seemed to be taking over the upper echelons of the London underworld undoubtedly inspired the Eastern European gangsters to push on with their 'invasion' plans for Kent, Essex and London via The Crossing.

* * *

The tentacles of many criminals operating in the UK spread ever further and wider following the murder of Russian gangster Misha, back in 2007. Many consider it was a pivotal turning point in the development of the UK as an unofficial crime state for foreign gangsters.

Vlad explained: 'There was a feeling that we could get away with anything after Misha was killed. We could do what the fuck we wanted in the UK and the police would never stand in our way.'

Kent armed robber Del put it more bluntly: 'The Russians got away with stuff because our government was scared shitless of them. It's their fault we're now in such a mess.'

The Crossing's role in the bizarre contract killing of Misha is admittedly tenuous, but there is no denying more than 100,000 lorry drivers thunder across Kent and Essex via The Crossing every single day of the week. The registration plates of those heavy goods vehicles come from dozens of different nations. The primary ones include Poland, Latvia, Serbia, Bulgaria, Romania and Albania to name but a few. And some of them will be filled with illegal contraband. After all, this is the most prized route into the crimelands of Britain.

As those trucks strain and crunch their gears to navigate the steep carriageways of the Queen Elizabeth II Bridge or entering the tunnel going under The Crossing in the opposite direction, it's worth remembering this is the UK.

* * *

At 11am on 24 August 2014, a foreign-registered articulated lorry caught fire in the early-morning mist as it crawled along in bumper-to-bumper traffic over The Crossing's Queen Elizabeth II Bridge. Motorists then stopped their vehicles to force the driver to open the back of the smoking trailer after he seemed hesitant to do so. With smoke still bellowing out of the roof of the lorry's trailer, motorists could hear the screams.

Inside that vehicle were thirteen illegal immigrants, some of whom had travelled across Europe from war-torn Syria.

The incident horrified police and citizens involved in the rescue because it brought home the reality of people smuggling. It was also a clear indication that the foreign gangs were here to stay.

In March 2016, Kent Police were called to a business park near The Crossing after reports that a lorry had been dumped. When they opened up the back of the vehicle, twenty-one Iranian and Iraqi adults and five children poured out. They were handed to Border Force officers.

One police officer later explained: 'Those poor people were being treated like a commodity. It turned out they'd been "sold" on three times since leaving Syria to ruthless criminals, who bartered with them as if they were goods in a marketplace.'

Foreign gangs today claim they turned to people smuggling because it enabled them to further finance their push for more territories in the homelands of Kent and Essex.

Alp Mehmet – from the campaign group Migration Watch UK – later said: 'This is genuinely concerning. It shows that while huge numbers of migrants are being stopped at the borders, significant numbers are getting through.'

Only occasionally do British naval or customs personnel come across vessels trying to cross the Channel to reach the UK.

'Most of these people smuggling operations are working because the authorities don't manage to catch them,' said one retired police officer.

Over the past few years, tens of thousands of people have been waiting in northern France for months at a time as they try to reach Britain, where they believe they will have a better chance of finding employment, according to French and British charities. These people often end up paying Eastern European gangsters thousands of euros to travel on a flimsy boat – frequently under perilous conditions – to the British mainland.

UK law enforcement agencies have no doubt this type of people smuggling is organised primarily by foreign gangsters based in Kent, usually within close reach of The Crossing.

When Calais coastguard organisation SNSM assisted in the rescue operation of one barely seaworthy RIB (Rigid Inflatable Boat) in May 2016, helicopters from England and France took part in the search. The passengers were eventually found floating helplessly in the RIB and were taken to the nearby port of Dover to be interviewed by Border Force officers.

'The castaways, who were migrants, had called their families, who then alerted the authorities and rescue missions were triggered on both sides of the Channel,' explained one Border Force official. 'This confirms our fears: the smugglers are willing to take extreme measures, but the Channel is a real highway, presenting a great danger for this type of crossing.'

On another occasion, rescuers were only alerted after one migrant made it back to the beach at Sangatte in northern France before dawn.

Officials believe that migrants from the infamous Jungle refugee camp in Calais were stepping up attempts to reach Britain until the closure of the camp in October 2016. There were even reports that Eastern European gangsters based in the UK had been touting their services inside the actual camp.

Back on dry land, people smugglers also continued to use lorries to enter the UK illegally. One Polish lorry driver recently claimed to have helped 3,000 migrants get into the UK illegally over a two-year period from his homeland. The Polish driver used The Crossing to move speedily through southeast England into the Essex countryside before cutting across country to join the A1 (M) motorway up to Lincolnshire, where many of the illegal migrants were found hard-labour jobs and secretly integrated into the tight-knit Polish communities who exist in that area.

* * *

During the later years of the last decade and into this decade, foreign gangs continued sweeping into areas close to The Crossing. One young Kent criminal called Michael explained to me: 'We started losing our territories to them. Our father's generation was encouraging us to hit back at the foreign gangs, but it wasn't easy or safe and they had much more firepower than us.'

He claimed that two of his closest friends were murdered by Eastern European gangsters soon after this war began, more than ten years ago: 'We never found their bodies but I am sure it was the Albanians. They was sending out a message to the British to back off.'

And it was clear this war raging over The Crossing had no rules or regulations. One foreign gangster told me: 'The Eastern Europeans are as hard on each other as they are on the Brits. If you cross them, then they come after you, whoever you are.'

A classic example came when a Romanian father was beaten to death in a side street near The Crossing by a gang armed with baseball bats. Sorin Serbu, thirty-six – allegedly a drugs and people trafficker – was at the centre of a brutal turf war. He'd only recently moved to the UK from Romania with his ten-year-old son.

Serbu had earlier made his fortune in drugs and prostitution rackets in Western Europe before moving across to Italy. He'd then travelled to the UK, where he had allegedly angered other Eastern European gangs already operating here.

Serbu was ambushed and attacked by a gang of eight hooded people, believed to also have been Romanian. He was later rushed to hospital but was pronounced dead shortly after.

Sources in Romania soon warned of further bloodshed associated with the murder of Serbu. They knew first hand how these type of turf wars end.

The newly arrived foreign gangs also had one undeniable advantage over the old-school British criminals: they were impossible for the police to infiltrate, which meant they were pretty much left to their own devices.

On the rare occasions when foreign criminals in the UK were exposed, it took an intricate police surveillance operation, often as not followed by a hairy cop car chase to bring any of the big fish to justice. A classic example was Albanian gang member Tristen Asllani, who in 2016 lost control of his BMW during a high-speed police chase in Crouch End, North London, and ploughed into a shop.

In the crumpled wreckage of the car, officers found a suit-case full of cocaine and later, at the twenty-nine-year-old's home, another 21kg of the drug and a Skorpion machine pistol with a silencer.

* * *

In the badlands of Kent and Essex the foreign gangsters' so-called pincer movement on the two counties had pretty much succeeded by 2012. Put simply, they had better and cheaper drugs to sell, they were always armed and their organisations were superbly well organised.

'We [are] very professional and proud of being efficient businessmen. That means selling good coke otherwise custom-ers go someplace else,' explained Albanian drug boss Bari.

'British gangs had been too greedy for too long before we got here. They cut coke with so much shit that it had no actual cocaine in it. That is stupid and short-sighted. We made sure there was real cocaine in stuff we sold on streets. Then customers come back for more and more. It makes good business sense, yes?'

As a result, the Eastern Europeans were taking over the recreational drugs supply business in entire towns and com-munities. They were also prepared to run other criminal enter-prises which the old school Brits 'turned their noses up at'.

Drugs spots in many areas of Kent, Essex and London became swamped with mainly Eastern European street dealers prepared to work longer and harder than their British counterparts.

'We'd have half-dozen street dealers covering [the] area the British gangsters would have covered with one dealer,' explained Bari. 'We also made sure we were always available by phone for customers, which means customers come back over and over again to buy more drugs. It's good business practice but many British criminals don't see this is a business and [it] has to be run like one.'

When one gang of British drug dealers decided to hit back at the foreign 'invaders' for daring to take over their drug spot territories in a number of Kent towns, it could only end one way.

Onetime professional criminal Kris explained: 'We turned up one day to find an Albanian fucker standing on our spot, selling drugs as if we'd given him permission. The trouble was he had a shooter and pointed it straight at us when we approached him.'

The following day, the British gang arrived at the same drugs spot armed with guns, knives and baseball bats.

Kris continues: 'We was gonna get them to leave, or so we thought. Well, when we turned up, their dealer wasn't even there. No one was around. We thought we'd won that battle without firing a bullet.'

But as three carloads of the British criminals headed home that night they were ambushed by a gang of Albanians – 'They forced us off the road and into a small field at gunpoint. I thought, this is it, we're gonna end up dead.

'They put all our weapons in the back of one of their vans. Then they started playing with us. One of them slashed at the neck of one of my mates with a knife while another foreigner put the barrel of his gun down my throat. It was fuckin' terrifying! They let us go in the end, but none of us ever had the bottle to hit back again. We closed down the drug-dealing operation, abandoned all our spots and split up for good. They'd won hands down.'

It was recently estimated that marijuana alone generated more than £3 billion a year in income for the foreign criminals based in south-east England – that is half of Albania's GDP.

* * *

On 20 March 2018, shoppers out with their families at the Stratford Centre, in East London, mostly looked the other way as a Romanian man was chased by a gang of four other Eastern Europeans through the busy shopping mall. The gang involved were already known to local shopkeepers and mall security staff as troublemakers who often 'patrolled' the centre, looking for victims.

Beniamin Pieknyi, twenty-one, had travelled to the shopping centre to meet a friend and, earlier, the pair had stopped to buy a bottle of water when Pieknyi was first set upon by the gang, who declared it was 'their area'.

Initially, a security guard had moved in to break up the fight, but a few minutes later as the pair left the centre, Pieknyi was cornered in a Subway fast food restaurant and subjected to an 'abhorrent' attack as his friend was held back.

A Latvian criminal called Vladyslav Yakymchuk, twenty-three, then stabbed Pieknyi in the chest with a long knife. He and four accomplices fled the scene as Pieknyi's friend and members of the public desperately tried to give first aid.

Yakymchuk was later jailed for a minimum of twenty-four years after pleading guilty to murder, violent disorder and possession of a bladed article at the Old Bailey.

The attack on Beniamin Pieknyi sparked a number of vicious attacks between Eastern European and Latvian criminals at flashpoints all over Kent, Essex and London in the following months. As Albanian drug lord Bari said: 'This kid was just out with a friend, Latvians had no right to attack him. Crazy motherfuckers!'

Ironically, many of these so-called crime-on-crime attacks and murders are being under-reported in the UK media because the majority of press attention revolves around the knife crime epidemic which has been sweeping London and many of England's big cities in recent years. However, some police and criminals are in no doubt that the knife attacks – primarily on black street gang members – are being fuelled by the invasion of the UK by the type of foreign criminals who have taken over areas near The Crossing.

One old-school British criminal called Jamie told me: 'The foreign boys not only started taking over our territory, but they also left a chilling legacy, thanks to their ultra-violent reputations.

'My son knew quite a few kids who were street dealers in East London and he says that a lot of knife crime attacks come down to the pressure these kids are under from the foreign gangsters to sell their drugs. This all makes sense to me. When kids are threatened by gun-toting gangsters, they're gonna turn more dangerous themselves and that's when they strike out.'

And in the midst of this appalling war, the much-feared Albanian Mafia – with ambitions to run the biggest drug operations in Britain – were secretly nurturing the Bulgarian Mafia in order to strengthen their powerbase, especially in London.

As drug lord Bari explained: 'We Albanians want to run everything and by linking up with Bulgarians, we made ourselves even more powerful in [the] UK underworld.'

But who were the bosses behind this surge in foreign gangsters invading the UK?

3

BIG FISH

'The Crossing works in both directions,' explained UK-based Albanian drug lord Bari. 'You come in on it, you commit crimes and then you get fuck outta there before no one even knows you here in first place!'

Bari had been introduced to me by a British criminal who is one of the few locals to get on with the Eastern Europeans. In his late-forties, he dresses like an English country gent and says he considers England to be his second home. He also happens to be just five feet tall.

Bari turned up for our first meeting in a brand-new black taxi cab which cost him £80,000. He explained: 'It's cool way to get around. No one suspects I use such a car and, in any case, they all look same to most people.'

The inside of the cab was equipped with a state-of-the-art television which served as a communication centre for Bari whenever he's working: 'This is like mobile office, then it's much harder for police to find us, you understand?'

Bari is probably the smallest gangster I've ever met, but he insisted this has never inhibited his rise to the top of gangsterdom.

'People know who I am and that's not such bad thing,' he explained. 'I been here long time and I understand the English. They had all this coming to them. They never took us seriously and now they pay the price.'

And there is no denying that the organisational skills of these mostly Eastern European professional gangs of criminals are second to none.

* * *

The distant, high-pitched 50cc engines sounded like neurotic sewing machines on heat as the noise of them bounced back and forth across the Thames Estuary as the omnipresent trucks climbed across the Queen Elizabeth II Bridge from north to south in the distance.

Less than half a mile away, on a vast, uneven stretch of wasteland close to the riverbank, a dozen scooters slipped and skidded across the muddy terrain. From a distance, it must have looked like a gang of errant teenagers, wearing helmets and practising for some kind of motorcross competition, except that each machine had a passenger riding pillion and all the scooters also had a pizza delivery box attached to the back. In fact, they were being trained to replicate the exact type of driving conditions they would experience out on a 'job' in the crimelands of London, where scooter raids on high-end businesses have virtually become a crime epidemic.

Many of the drivers spun their scooters in 360-degree turns while others sped precariously across the uneven surface of that wasteland. Some used small ridges in the terrain to bounce off the ground before landing with a thump and continuing their manic driving routines as their passengers held on for dear life.

Watching all this was a man in his late-thirties with a slight foreign accent known as Toni. We had been introduced by pint-sized Bari, who proudly announced that Toni had once been a football star, back home in Albania.

Toni isn't his real name. He's called that because of the scar he has across his left cheek, which reminded his associates of Tony Montana, the character played with such venom by Al Pacino in the movie *Scarface*. It is just about the most popular film ever made for an authentic gangster audience.

As the scooters continued their manic 'dance' around the wasteland, the young helmeted pilots and their passengers held on tightly while pushing their two-wheel machines to the absolute limit.

'They have to handle these scooters properly before I allow them to go out on jobs,' Toni explained as we stepped a few feet to our left to avoid being knocked over by one scooter as it slewed past, leaving a trail of dust in its wake.

The 'jobs' he was referring to were multiple smash 'n' grab raids on high-end shops in London's West End. Over the past ten years, these dramatic crimes have been caught on CCTV video footage on many occasions, but thanks to helmets that disguise the participants, the police have failed to stamp out this crime phenomenon.

Off in the distance away from this riverside wasteland, hundreds of vehicles were using The Crossing to travel back and forth over the estuary, most of them blissfully unaware that these boys and their machines were out training for a life of crime in much the same way as African child soldiers train for war.

'These kids don't just get on a scooter and carry out a robbery. They have to be trained to deal with all sorts of situations, otherwise they'd soon get caught. Also, having passengers can really destabilise [a] scooter. It has to be driven in a completely different way, so this type of training is very important,' Toni told me.

A few minutes later, he ordered all his young pupils to stop and gather round us: time for a pep talk. All of them kept their helmets on. Clearly, Toni and his protégés didn't want any outsiders to be able to later identify them.

'Right,' he shouted to the scooter boys, 'I want all your keys now!'

The scooter boys dutifully stepped forward and threw their keys into a cardboard box on the ground.

'You,' said Toni, nodding at one particularly skinny teenager whose helmet seemed far too big compared to the rest of his body, 'get one of them started. Now!'

Toni pressed on a stopwatch.

The scooter boy scrambled swiftly across the muddy terrain, pulled a machine to its feet and flipped the stand bar up. Then he began poking around just beneath the handlebars. Seconds later, he kick-started the machine into life.

'Excellent,' said Toni. 'Now, rest of you do it. Now!'

Most of them had their machines up and running without the use of a key within less than two minutes on Toni's stopwatch. But two of the youths were still struggling when he said: 'Time's up.'

He looked across at the pair.

'Come back when you know how to do it,' he said dismissively.

Still wearing their helmets, they slouched off.

* * *

Ten minutes later, I was with Toni in a shipping container converted into an office, close to The Crossing. He explained: 'I get kids coming here every day, asking if they can join scooter gangs, but you gotta test them out first. Many are useless. Better to find that out now than when they're in a middle of job.'

These type of scooter gangs have become an integral part of the UK's new underworld, especially throughout the badlands of Kent, Essex and London. In the past ten years, it's estimated that hundreds of raids have been carried out in London and the South-East and those robberies have netted criminals upwards of £20 million.

Just then, two more would-be scooter boys walked in for a meeting with Toni. One was the nephew of a Romanian drug lord, the other was the son of one of Albania's most-feared drug smugglers. They seemed young, barely out of their teens, yet Toni explained that more than five years earlier, they'd been members of a scooter gang who carried out a phenomenally successful series of smash 'n' grab raids in the West End of London.

'These two have graduated now. They no longer work on scooters, but they very good so they come and help me find the new "stars",' explained Toni, refusing to elaborate further. He then changed the subject back to how he organised the scooter boys' gangs for their raids into Central London: 'We plan targets carefully and even talk through escape routes – all the shortcuts, both there and back. I run professional outfit and only way we can succeed is to be disciplined and organised.'

* * *

'Organisation – that's what they had, which we hadn't.'

Terry, a legendary 'face', as they used to call criminals in the south of England, is one of the UK's oldest-living gangsters. He admitted stepping back completely as the foreign gangs began to win those turf wars in Essex and Kent.

He believes that the massive influx of foreign gangsters into Britain was 'inevitable' and explained: 'It pains me to fuckin' say it, but they knew what they was doin' from the get-go. Most British villains are a mess. They don't run their gangs like corporations, they're either drunk or off their heads on coke, or both.

'But most of the foreign lads hardly ever touch a drop of the hard stuff. They're workaholics and they knew there would be many openings when it comes to the crime game in this country.'

Terry says one of the turning points in the war between the local gangsters and the foreigners came when the Albanians led the charge into the area in and around The Crossing.

'That was the clincher. By taking over this territory, they got themselves a free ride into Essex and the north of London. I know of one Bulgarian fella who drives in pounds of coke every month from Eastern Europe. He once told me he could get from his home in Sofia to North London in under twenty-four hours by car. A lot of that is down to The Crossing.'

But there is one side to the foreign gangs which even Terry has a problem with:

'They don't care about using kids to work for them and that's out of order in my book,' he said. 'That's like something out of Charles Dickens. It ain't right!

'I knew one Romanian villain who had five teams of scooter gangs operating in the centre of London, carrying out smash 'n' grab raids on jewellers and stuff like that. These kids – they was no more than sixteen, I reckon – had to drive themselves back to base south of The Crossing, near Dartford. That Romanian ran that place like he was a real-life Fagin. He kicked those kids around and paid them as little as possible and they was taking all the risks for him.'

It sounded just like Toni's operation. In fact, one of London's most notorious scooter gangs still operating to this day was even nicknamed Fagin's Kitchen Crew because of the way these young criminals were treated by their foreign gangmasters.

British criminal Terry added: 'A lot of these kids are shipped over from Eastern Europe, made to sleep two to a bed in a shithole property or a shipping container and treated like dirt. That Romanian villain I knew didn't give a toss about them. He didn't really care if they lived or died, just so long as they brought him in loads of money.'

And it's not just Eastern Europeans who are responsible for the scooter gangs now plaguing London's streets.

One of the most notorious scooter gangs in recent years was run and manned by Ecuadorians. Their operation only became exposed to the world when a teenage scooter driver was shot by police during a chase.

The victim turned out to be the son of an old-school London-born gangster, who rode with the gang. The father was so upset he broke the underworld 'golden rule' and informed on the South Americans and the gang was eventually caught by the police.

As former British criminal Terry explained: 'That shows you how bad things had got.'

Meanwhile, more scooter gangs continue to emerge regularly, often replacing the ones caught by the police.

During the early days of this so-called underworld war, the old school gangsters laughed at the scooters, which they considered to be 'girls toys'.

'That was yet another fuckin' mistake by us. We thought we was cleverer than them and the opposite was true,' Terry conceded.

Often foreign gangs only use one scooter with a passenger for certain 'special jobs' because it attracts less attention. A classic example came back a few years ago when two teenagers on a stolen Aprilia scooter – wearing silver and black helmets – screeched to a halt outside an electronics shop in Central London at 1.34am. Within minutes, they had grabbed a sledgehammer from the back of their bike, smashed their way into the store and made off with more than £200,000 worth of electrical equipment.

In the nineteenth century, the original Fagin would have sent out his ragamuffin kids to pick the pockets of London gentlemen. Today, the kids are forced into selecting richer pickings, from the jewellery boutiques of Bond Street to the hi-fi shops along Tottenham Court Road and the designer clothes stores in the West End and the Square Mile of the City of London. But as rival foreign criminal gangs moved in to earn millions from these smash 'n' grab raids, police feared these scooter boys would start arming themselves to the teeth in order to see off their rivals, striking even more fear into any potential targets.

On social media, some London scooter gangs became so cocky and confident that they posted footage of themselves celebrating their activities around the housing estates in North London where many of them were based. One piece of much-circulated footage showed them racing in the streets, performing wheelies and lighting aerosol cans as one of their leaders chanted a rap song in the background.

But most teenage London scooter gangs operate in groups of four to six, using Italian scooters with the number plates obscured.

'They come into the City at night down the backways and alleys to avoid CCTV cameras. They usually operate between 12 and 2am and ride pillion,' one police detective explained. 'They're ruthless, they smash their way into a store and within two minutes, they are gone. Sometimes they even have back-up in 4x4 vehicles.

'There is a huge network of them, and they change crews around all the time, which makes it more difficult to catch them.

'They know what they are stealing – they go for watches worth £400,000 and light goods like laptops. They are getting rid of the stuff straight away and that does not involve them selling it down the pub.'

Many police officers are reluctant to chase the scooter boys too hard in case they force the drivers into head-on collisions, which could end in serious, life-changing injuries or even death.

'The police are often inhibited from chasing down the scooter boys in case they get hurt and that is also helping these young villains get away,' explained one recently retired officer.

Back in 2006, when scooter raids first began, many store holders in Central London accused the police of not taking the raids seriously enough. But in recent years there has been much less criticism as it has become clear the police really do care.

In the City of London – where many of the raids have taken place – police introduced their own scooters to try and pursue the robbers. In one incident, a gang member threw a club hammer at a police officer on a scooter and he was almost seriously injured. His machine was completely written off.

CCTV footage from one recent scooter raid showed the brutal efficiency of the teenage boys as they sledgehammered the windows and used bolt-cutters to breach the shutters of a store front. At one point an off-duty policeman – who was drinking in a nearby bar – was seen rushing at the teenagers with a bar stool, forcing them to drop thousands of pounds worth of equipment. But the gang got away, as is so often the case.

A friend of mine who lives in the Kent countryside a short distance from The Crossing told me recently that he was driving home late at night on the M20 motorway when he encountered a gang of scooter boys.

'They were driving in front of me across all three lanes of the motorway in formation, a bit like fighter jets. It was an awesome, bizarre sight and they didn't even feel obliged to let me past when they realised I was behind them.

'I decided not to hoot them in case they turned nasty but I also had a sneaking admiration for them. I don't really know why, but there was something impressive about them – they seemed to have no fear whatsoever.'

The foreign gangs are clearly here to stay.

Toni – who has trained many scooter gangs over recent years – revealed: 'The scooter boy gangs were first invented in Romania and Albania because most young criminals couldn't afford cars, so they started using scooters for robberies. But we soon realised that here in the UK were many much richer people and places so we [the Albanians] split up areas of Central London with the Romanians because it is perfect for using scooters for robberies.'

In fact, his scooter boys often use special radio transmitters so they can talk to each other through headphones incorporated in their helmets during a raid.

He went on: 'The British gangsters didn't even think of committing crimes this way. They live in the past, still thinking masked men with shotguns in vans are the only way to rob a jewellery store.'

Back at the shipping container where Toni runs a variety of businesses based in the shadow of The Crossing's Queen Elizabeth II Bridge, he also revealed that he used another huge shipping container as a hub for 'hot' cars driven by Eastern European gangsters, in and out of the UK. Some years back, the Albanians, Romanians, Bulgarians and a small group of Latvians clubbed together to open this secretive 'business' where stolen cars can speedily switch their licence plates.

'The police on The Crossing electronically monitor every vehicle and for years this caused us a lot of problems. Many gangsters would be picked up by police a few miles either side of The Crossing after their number plates flagged up as fake,' he explained.

The foreign gangsters' drive-in 'centre' enables them to switch number plates almost as quickly as Grand Prix racing drivers change tyres during a pitstop.

'You come in here, pay a fee and then the car plates are immediately changed by a mechanic. We have a guy here twenty-four hours a day. He lives in an apartment near The Crossing.

Now, those cars the police see with false plates using The Crossing literally "disappear" before police have time to stop vehicle.'

As I was talking to Toni, the metal entrance gates to the car park enclosed by high mesh fencing were opened by one of his men. A man in sunglasses, driving a top-of-the-range BMW coupé, roared in. Less than five minutes later, he had exchanged a wad of cash for new plates and departed.

Toni told me: 'A few years back, we all agreed to put some money into pot to set up this place. It has worked well. If anyone comes asking, we make out it is mobile garage for normal mechanical problems. I'm certain police know we have system in place, but they don't have the manpower to set up a road block every time they think false plates have been used on a car on The Crossing.'

Back at the same enclosed car park, Toni told how – although most of his family were still living near the Albanian capital Tirana – he spends more than half the year in a modest council flat on a housing estate just near The Crossing. The flat is sublet from a genuine council tenant who lives in Spain.

'Listen, I have the big house, the big car, the blingy rings, you name it, back in Albania. But here, I stay low-key and no one bothers me. I'm invisible, I don't exist in eyes of the law.

'I look like a nobody and that's the way I wanna keep it. I dress down. My flat is a shithole. Trust me, all my neighbours don't have a clue who I am.'

Toni was actually brought up for half his childhood in an area just south of The Crossing because his Albanian father married a local girl after he was granted political asylum, back in the mid-1970s.

'The old man had links to the political party opposed to Albania's communist rulers at that time, so he did have real reasons for leaving Albania. But he also had many friends who were in Albanian underworld, which he never mentioned to the British authorities at the time.

'My dad left many of his family back in Albania and gradually they started moving here. He even worked with a few old-time British criminals back when he arrived here. But he fell out with them because they treated him like shit – they hated all foreigners.'

From the mid-1990s for around ten years, Toni claims his father was the most powerful foreign criminal in the south-east of England.

'He was one of the first and the British gangsters kept threatening to kill him because they hated foreigners. But my dad didn't care. He was much cleverer than them and whenever they tried to get him, he'd hit them back even harder.

'But then one day my dad decided he'd had enough so he divorced my mum, moved back to Albania, bought himself a big house and a new woman and lived there until the day he died.'

Toni prides himself on being 'low-key' and is convinced it has helped him avoid arrest in the UK *and* problems with local criminals.

'Some foreign gangsters here flash their wealth around. That is stupid. They just don't get it – the police here will stop you if they just see you in an expensive car.'

He stays 'under the radar' by often travelling everywhere on one of those same pizza delivery scooters he stores in another shipping container for scooter robbery training sessions.

'Nobody notices a guy in a helmet on a scooter on his own. I can get places much faster and you know what? There is no toll charge for using The Crossing on one. That means the police don't electronically monitor my scooter like they do all the vehicles that are charged for using The Crossing.'

Half an hour later, he showed me into his 'shithole' flat on the ground floor of a rundown tower block so close to The Crossing that you could hear the omnipresent traffic thundering over the Queen Elizabeth II Bridge. One room was filled with boxes of stolen watches and jewellery. On the main dining table was a counting machine where Tony added up the value of his scooter gangs' stolen goods, like a modern-day Fagin.

Just then there was a knock at the door: it was two youths in their late teens.

'What d'you want?' barked Toni.

'You owe us from that last job,' one of them said nervously.

'Fuck off and come back tomorrow! I'll have some cash then.'

The boys didn't argue and left, tails firmly between their legs.

Toni explained: 'I gotta be careful with these kids because it only takes one of them talking and I'll have the cops on my back.'

Then he opened a drawer in a cupboard and produced a revolver.

'Sometimes I leave this out when I'm dealing with these kids, so they know not to fuck me around.'

'What happens if they go on a robbery and it doesn't work out and they come back with nothing?' I asked.

'That depends,' he said. 'If they've fucked up big time and left clues behind then I tell 'em to disappear. But not before I make 'em realise that if they talk to anyone, not just the cops, then I will come after them.'

Toni claims the traditional Central London high-end luxury store targets for the scooter boys are just as easy to steal from as they were ten years ago: 'You'd think they'd tighten up on security a bit, wouldn't you? Well, I can tell you, it's still fuckin' easy pickings.'

Then, as an after-thought, he added: 'The best thing of all is that all my boys have helmets, they are not identifiable. How sweet is that? CCTV means fuck-all to us! You can't see the faces of my boys because of the helmets and the scooters are either stolen or have false plates or both.'

Toni's mobile phone starts ringing. He answers it after carefully studying the caller ID first.

'How did it go?'

'Excellent!'

* * *

The following day, Toni introduced me to one of his 'star' scooter 'pilots', twenty-two-year-old Darren. He actually hails from an old-school British criminal family from Essex, but insisted he had no problems working for Eastern European mobsters like Toni.

Darren explained: 'I've been doing this sorta work since I was sixteen. My mum and dad and brothers think I'm stupid to trust the foreign gangsters, but they've never done me no harm. I've earned a lot of cash from the raids – a lot more than the rest of my family have from crime – I reckon they're a bit jealous of my success.'

He believes that the war between the old-school British gangsters and these so-called 'new kids on the bloc' would never have happened if they'd all sat down and tried to talk to each other in the first place.

'It's all about trust, ain't it?' he explained. 'Two of my best mates are Albanians living here and I'd trust them with my life. But if I told my old man that he'd go ballistic. But the old boys like my dad need to realise these fellas are here for keeps.'

Darren's 'boss' Toni is full of praise for him too: 'He's a good kid. He knows his job backwards now and I hope we can hold onto him because he's also very good at giving advice to the new scooter kids who come into this game.'

In this flat on a housing estate just a stone's throw from The Crossing, Toni explained proudly why he believed he and so many Eastern Europeans have integrated so seamlessly into such communities: 'I respect people on this estate and most of the residents know to keep quiet about us. They'd rather have us here than a bunch of crackheads, which is what they had before we arrived.'

He also revealed that the Eastern European gangsters operating in these parts never use the Channel Tunnel because it is so well monitored by police and customs due to fears of a terrorist attack.

'Some hotheads can't understand why we live and operate so close to The Crossing. But, believe me, it's better this way. I need to always know what's going on. I also know that if there is an emergency, I can drive back to Albania in less than twenty-four hours.'

* * *

Within a few years of the Tonbridge cash depot heist back in 2006, Eastern European gangsters had succeeded in throwing most of the British criminals out of their own Kent and Essex 'backyards'. They had set up uber-efficient 'businesses' covering a wide range of criminal enterprises.

'Most of the old-school Brits gave up the fight,' robber Teddy explained. 'There is no other way to describe it. We were facing a bunch of psychos and it wasn't worth it.

'The foreigners ended up pushing most of us out of our territories almost as far as the sea. In the end, the closest the Brits could get to The Crossing was going with their families to those shopping malls near both sides of The Crossing.'

When one British gang tried to ambush a gang of Albanians in a darkened street on an industrial estate near The Crossing 'to put them in their place', it provoked a chilling response from the Eastern Europeans.

Bari explained: 'We didn't want no problems but the old British guys started to kick up trouble, so we teach them a few lessons.' He refused to elaborate but it's rumoured two members of that British gang were never seen again after 'going for a swim'.

In 2012, some Eastern European gangs in Kent and Essex joined forces once more to deliberately provoke the few remaining 'troublesome' English gangs by committing some outrageous crimes right on their doorstep. They decided to target those shopping malls near The Crossing, which the British gangsters looked on as their own 'family-friendly' territories. Their first 'assault' was on the Lakeside shopping mall in Essex, just a few miles north of The Crossing. It was renowned as a 'safe' place where British gangsters often went with their families.

A gang of Romanian criminals robbed a Goldsmiths jewellery store inside the mall shortly before 10.30am on Thursday, 19 July 2012. After threatening staff with a hammer and an axe, they forced them to hand over more than thirty Breitling, Cartier and Rolex watches valued at almost £170,000.

CCTV footage showed the men forcing their way through locked doors and metal shutters before throwing their haul into holdalls while one stood as lookout, ready to throw Molotov cocktails, should they be disturbed.

A female member of staff at the jewellery store in Lakeside suffered minor injuries during the attack, but did not require any medical treatment. Other staff were shocked by the incident, which sparked a search of the area by armed police and the police helicopter.

The three raiders – who all wore dark clothing with hoodies and scarves across their faces – escaped in a black Audi A1 hatchback. A few hours after the robbery, the car was found abandoned some miles away; it had originally been stolen from a business in West London.

'We were telling Brits that we could strike anywhere. Any place if we wished,' Albanian drug lord Bari later explained.

The following day, another jewellery store was hit by raiders at the nearby Bluewater Shopping Centre on the other Kent side of The Crossing. This time £1.2 million worth of goods was stolen.

'It told them a simple message,' said Bari. 'We run this territory now, not you.'

At least another half dozen more robberies at the same two shopping centres followed. On some occasions the robbers even left an extra calling card by torching vehicles and setting tyres alight as a distraction and to hinder the emergency services.

'The British don't do that so we knew it was the Eastern European gangsters,' added British criminal Rob. 'We was overwhelmed by those fuckers, they was everywhere.'

DCI Stuart Smith – who led the Essex Police investigation into the raids – told reporters afterwards: 'National borders no longer stop criminals from committing crimes internationally and in the same way as British criminals commit crime on the Continent, here we had Romanian criminals committing crime in Essex.'

Veteran Essex criminal Kenny Fowler explained: 'The Eastern Europeans deliberately targeted Lakeside over and over again to wind us up because it's the place where we shop with our families. It felt as if the foreign gangs were putting two fingers up at us and saying nowhere is sacred as far as they are concerned. It was outrageous.'

During another later robbery at Bluewater, a team of eight raiders targeted a Breitling watch store in the middle of the night. They were only foiled after being filmed by a CCTV camera, which the gang had not seen.

'The Romanians were behind that one, too,' recalled criminal Vince. 'They were all playing with us, telling us to give up whatever territory they still had.

'Don't get me wrong, the lads who did that job were very professional but it upset a lot of the locals because this was a foreign team on what was once our territory. It was bang out of order.'

Old-school British criminal Billy Lacey explained: 'Bluewater is actually much more dangerous than Lakeside, a lot more dodgy people use it than Lakeside. I read somewhere it is the fourth biggest crime hotspot in England and Wales. That says it all.'

* * *

Today, Romanians are the second largest community of foreigners living in Britain, with over 413,000 living and working in the UK. Ten years ago, Britain's Romanian population stood at 42,000 – a tenfold increase in just a decade.

Nowhere is that more apparent than in Burnt Oak – a London suburb where Romanian is the second most commonly spoken language, and where 56 per cent of school-age children don't even speak English as a first language. As many as 35 per cent of immigrants living in Burnt Oak come from Romania and the area, with its Romanian shops, restaurants and even a church which offers services in Romanian, is frequently referred to as 'Bontoc'.

Pint-sized Albanian 'godfather' Bari has been operating as a criminal in the UK for over ten years and has always made it clear he's here to stay. Bari insists the Eastern European gangs had 'no choice' but to crush the old school criminals who once ruled London, Kent and Essex.

'When I first came to UK, the British criminals were not interested. They saw themselves as "above" what we do, especially the prostitution and people smuggling. But the British criminals brought this on themselves. They were badly organised and we recognised this quickly so we set out to destroy anyone who got in [the] way. This strategy worked well because we were stronger than them.'

* * *

In 2014, a gang of ruthless and much-feared Ukrainian gangsters began circling the area close to The Crossing, already under the control of a joint team of other Eastern European criminals. This gang of immensely wealthy Ukrainian ex-servicemen was known as The Odessa Boys, after the town in southern Ukraine where they all originally came from. They had an audacious plan to cash in on the 'profitability' of the area.

Albanian drug lord Bari explained: 'These fuckin' Ukrainians had lot of cash and they try to buy up much land close to Thames to develop it. They thought they could clean all their black money and make fat profit. But they were asking for trouble because cops could see they were loaded. And at same time they were taunting us, trying to prove they had biggest balls – bad move!'

Albanian scooter raid boss Toni explained: 'Yeah, I heard about Odessa Boys and how they tried to buy property here. My uncle said they were nothing compared to another gang of Ukrainians who tried to set up a crime network here, more than twenty years ago.'

That earlier gang were known as 'Angert's Gang' and had arrived in Britain in the late-1990s with a reputation for extortion and murdering their enemies.

'Back in those days, the British criminals still running Kent and Essex smashed Angert's Gang into pieces,' said Toni. 'In the end, they were either killed or ran back to Ukraine.'

However, he is convinced that 'Angert's Gang' left a twisted legacy which has worked to the advantage of many Eastern European gangs ever since.

'The new Ukrainian gang who turned up here did not realise we were the power brokers around The Crossing, not the

British. They thought they could come in here and take over everything.'

But nothing could have been further from the truth.

* * *

Since the Eastern European gangsters first arrived in large numbers in the UK fifteen years ago, many of them have based themselves in overcrowded council housing estates across Central London, as well as in the Home Counties.

'The more overcrowded, the better for us,' explained Bari. 'That way, no one notices us. Many people on these estates have something to hide themselves, so they not want to help police. That's why we move into them.'

No wonder Albanian is today said to be the second language spoken on many housing estates in London and the south-east of England. At one such rundown concrete jungle in East London, an Albanian youth gang called the Hellbanianz even have their own unofficial UK 'headquarters'. The Hellbanianz's teams of street drug dealers are renowned throughout London for their violence and are so brazen they often put photos of their Ferraris and other supercars onto social media, along with pictures of their gang members holding wads of £50 notes and gold Rolex watches.

Before the gang's account was closed in November 2018, Hellbanianz had 115,000 Instagram followers. They even produced a music video called *Hood Life*, which opened with a drone shot of the estate where their headquarters was located. The lyrics discuss defending their territories of London with 'kallash' (AK47s) – and dishing out threats to a rival Albanian gang called OTR (On Top Of The Rest) and a fair few others.

Another video recently released openly stated they were 'ready for war'.

Many other criminals believe that the Hellbanianz gang deliberately posts footage on social media to try and lure 'falcons' – fresh recruits – with shots of scantily clad women, wheel-spinning Bentleys and the ubiquitous wads of money.

A teenage resident on one particular housing estate recently dubbed the Hellbanianz gangsters 'the stabbers'. Requesting anonymity, this resident recalled: 'You'd be walking home and feel a little prick on your leg and, later, you realised you'd been stabbed by one of the Albanian kids.'

Hellbanianz members themselves openly admit having moved onto housing estates because of their close proximity to Central London, The Crossing and the channel ports. As one member of the gang told me: 'It was the perfect place for us. We come and go between here and Albania.'

The Hellbaniaz are considered by many older Albanian criminals to be lower-level gangsters, working the streets as drug dealers and enforcers for the bigger, older Albanian Mafia syndicate in London and the south-east known as the Shqiptare, who've been instrumental in flooding the UK with billions of pounds worth of cocaine over the past ten years.

Not surprisingly, the young – mainly under thirty – criminals of the Hellbaniaz are considered by many older criminals to be out-of-control 'psychos'. One Essex criminal – Vic – told me: 'They're fuckin' nutters. They even boast about it all on Facebook and I can tell you, none of the usual Brit faces would ever take them on. They're vicious, they're not worth it.'

Hellbanianz's high-profile lifestyle has fostered increasing tensions within the Albanian community, particularly the blatant goading of police. One early video put online showed gang members surrounding a Met Patrol car.

Albanian career criminal Qasim explained: 'This goes against the Albanian culture. Some of the older criminals, international traders, didn't like this behaviour. It exposed their activities by putting the police under pressure to break up the gangs. The traditional Albanian gangsters wanted to remain low-key, making profits without being caught.'

Longridge Road in Barking, Essex – a short hop from The Crossing – is home to numerous Albanian restaurants. It's a place where the young hoods from Hellbanianz are not welcome. Many customers scowl when the gang or names of prominent members are mentioned, others completely deny its existence. But as long as Albanian mobsters from the old school Shqiptare Mafia keep delivering their cocaine to the street dealers of London and elsewhere, recruiting teenagers to the Hellbanianz gang will always be easy.

The Albanian Mafia's contribution to the biggest crime wave the UK has ever known is a result of combining the 'traditional' characteristics of rigid internal discipline with a clan structure, great reliability and a commercially aware network to sell on contraband.

The Albanians positively thrive on complicated logistics operations, which require them to deliver drugs almost everywhere in the UK and always on time. No wonder their remarkable ability to integrate within communities enabled them to exploit all criminal opportunities.

In many ways, these Albanian Mafia groups are hybrid organisations capable of financing themselves from all sorts of different sources. The typical structure of the Albanian Mafia is hierarchical. A family clan is referred to as a 'fis' or a 'fare'. Families contain an executive committee known as a 'Bajrak' and select a high-ranking member for each unit. A unit is led by a 'krye' or 'boss', who selects 'kryetar' or 'underbosses' to serve under them. The kryetar will then choose a 'mik' or 'friend', who acts as a liaison to members and is responsible for coordinating unit activities.

The Albanian Mafia term 'besa' means trust and is the name attached to their 'Code of Honour'. During the gang recruitment process a member inducted into the Albanian Mafia is required to take an oath. The oath is then considered sacred because it is defined as a Besë.

Besa is extremely important in Albanian culture and is considered a verbal contract of trust, especially in Northern Albania. When somebody gives someone their Besë, they have pledged their life and are going to protect them with their life.

Albanian gangster Bari explained: 'That promise is [an] important part of the ancestral code of Kanun. This says that member does have right to take revenge. That means blood must be paid with blood. In other words, "Only trust those similar to you".'

Today, Albanians are the third largest foreign nationality locked up in UK prisons despite only tens of thousands living in the UK, compared to almost a million Poles.

* * *

Back at The Crossing, Eastern European gangs still found themselves facing occasional incursions by the small pockets of British criminals who hadn't yet surrendered this prime territory.

Enter The Warrior – a specialist hitman who builds bombs and often disguises murders as terror attacks. Bari explained: 'Warrior sometimes gets called in here to finish off the Brits when they are pissing us off.' But he insisted this was only as a last resort and that most of the few remaining British criminals eventually proposed a so-called 'peace treaty': 'We decided to accept the Brits' suggestion of peace. Maybe that was a mistake, maybe they will one day come back to kill us, but we not want to kill people just for [the] sake of it.'

No one will publicly reveal the details of this so-called 'peace treaty' but it seems to have led to a halt in the bloodshed – for the moment.

* * *

Albanian criminals based in the UK are extremely clever diplomats, as well as opportunists. Soon after consolidating territories throughout Kent and Essex and agreeing that peace treaty, they went into partnership with a gang of Turks based in the Essex coastal resort of Southend-on-Sea. The Turks controlled the heroin trade in the UK at the time and still do to this day. Then there was the 'vice business' – which most English professional criminals had ignored for years. The Albanian gangs had no such qualms about raking in cash from sex for sale.

Vice squad officers at Scotland Yard today estimate that Albanians now control more than 75 per cent of the UK's brothels and their operations in London's Soho alone are said to be worth more than £15 million a year.

Albanian gangsters have a presence in every big city in Britain, as well as many smaller towns and communities. They're also not afraid to fight off rival criminals in vicious turf wars, if necessary. Associate groups within all Eastern European criminal organisations in the UK often hide their nefarious activities within restaurants, bars and clubs in an attempt to remain unexposed. But it is the *real* identity of many Eastern European gangsters operating in the UK which most concerns law enforcement agencies. One Scotland Yard drugs squad detective told me: 'The trouble is they all come here on false passports. We haven't a clue who most of them really are. Some come here to the UK to escape authorities back home in places like Albania, where they're often wanted for a vast range of crimes. Then they settle here under new identities, often applying for and getting UK passports.'

Several factors help explain why organised crime was able to put down such strong roots in Albania long before their gangs made it to the UK. One reason was the disbanding in 1991 – after the fall of communism – of the country's security service, the Sigurimi, which then left around 10,000 unemployed agents with skills well-suited to organised crime. There was also the collapse six years later of various Albanian pyramid pension schemes, which robbed many people of their life savings and prompted the looting of more than 550,000 small arms from military armouries. Then there was the emergence in Albania and Kosovo during the Balkan Wars of strong links between criminals, politicians and guerrilla fighters (with some players filling all three roles).

By the late-1990s, territories – especially in northern Albania, where clan loyalties had always been strongest – had become violent, lawless places, riven by murderous feuds. Many Eastern European criminals claim to have moved to the UK to get away from violence and corruption in their home countries. Certainly, most of those countries were a lot more dangerous to live in than the UK.

The northern Albanian town of Burrel, for example, had become known as the country's murder capital after no fewer than 150 people were brutally slain there in a single year in the late-1990s. The killing spree erupted when two rival gangs fought for control of the territory. They were named after the local families who ran them: the Kolas and the Dedas. After looting a munitions store, the gangs armed themselves with rocket-launchers, grenades and machine-guns. A shootout ensued and two men were eventually charged with attempted murder.

As Albanian drug lord Bari explained: 'What happened in Burrel is exactly what could happen here in England, where the Albanians have settled. We all know that in the end a gun speaks many words.'

A classic example of the type of characters who have illicitly slipped across the UK border was one-legged Albanian career criminal Avni Metra, now in his fifties, who first arrived in Britain back in 1998 and was given a UK passport after claiming to be a Kosovan war refugee. Earlier in Albania, he had allegedly gouged out one man's eyes and cut off the ears of another murder victim. While the man writhed on the ground, pleading for mercy, Metra riddled his body with bullets.

During the mid-nineties, back in Albania, Metra even served as the henchman for a Mafia-style gang who took over an isolated mountain community amid an orgy of bloodshed, plundering banks and businesses, and even raping local women.

Wearing a green military greatcoat – beneath which he concealed a Kalashnikov machine-gun looted from an army weapons store – witnesses later recalled how Metra would open fire without a second thought on anyone who stood in the gang's way.

He had eventually been convicted of two murders in Albania in 1995, but authorities in the UK were unaware of this when Metra set up home in leafy Borehamwood, Hertfordshire, in the heart of Middle England. He had actually paid £5,000 to a criminal gang to facilitate his trip to the UK and escape justice. In 1999, his wife and young child joined him from Albania, after posing as Kosovan refugees.

Metra soon controlled an Albanian prostitution racket in London and quickly rose to the top of the Albanian Mafia in the UK despite his wanted status back in his home country.

Interpol chiefs in the Albanian capital Tirana have always claimed they requested Metra's arrest back in 2008 after they learned he'd settled in London, but they were informed that British police could not find him.

In 2010, Metra was even arrested and charged with domestic violence against his wife. He was only given a twelve-month restraining order.

In fact, UK detectives did not realise that Metra – using the bogus name Avdul Mekra – was a notorious fugitive. It was only in 2018 that he was finally brought to justice and extradited back to Albania.

Meanwhile, Interpol continued to urge UK police to find one of Metra's evil fellow gang members, who was said to have bribed his way out of prison in Tirana after being convicted of the same two murders as Metra and receiving a similar twenty-five-year sentence.

This second killer was in fact hiding in northern England using a false Kosovan identity. More pertinently, a relative of his in Albania later told a British newspaper that many members of this man's family had settled in the UK, too. He has never been located.

Saliman Barci, forty-one, was another one of thousands of others who arrived in the UK claiming to be a Kosovan refugee. Even though he was a cocaine dealer, he was given a four-bed council house and £2,000 a month in benefits. He also had a prosthetic limb fitted by the NHS.

* * *

Albanian drug lord Bari admitted that gangs of youths like the Hellbaniaz are vital cogs in the machinery of the Albania Mafia in the UK: 'The cocaine market here in UK is dominated by us Albanians now. It comes in through trucks and on ships in the Thames, which carry containers.'

He then revealed that the Albanians recently secured a new deal to get all their cocaine direct from Colombian and Peruvian cartels in the way the Romanian Mafia had managed some years earlier. This was through the Albanian crime syndicate the Shqiptare. Their connections to the notorious Ndrangheta Italian Mafia cartel helped convince the South Americans to deal directly with the Albanians after falling out with the Romanians, who had had the exclusive 'rights' to import cocaine directly from Colombia and other cocaine-producing countries at that time.

The Italian Ndrangheta clan controlled most of mainland Europe's cocaine trade by this stage and these two potent criminal organisations constantly 'discussed new projects', which included sending even more gangs into the UK. The Albanians in the UK recognised very early on that cocaine was restricted by its complex sales process. Importers worked separately from wholesalers and the gangs who sold cocaine on the street were often the tenth or even twelth organisation to handle the drug.

Bari explained: 'This means price always changing depending on purity and this put off customers. That's why Albanians went to the Ndrangheta to get permission to deal direct with the Colombians. By agreeing all shipments of coke would come direct from South America, supply chains were kept in-house.'

The Albanians eventually showed extraordinary business acumen in securing their cocaine for just £5,000 a kilo directly from the South Americans compared to £22,500 a kilo they had been paying a Dutch wholesaler who had previously supplied them with the drug after they fell out with the Romanians.

The Albanians once again made another extremely radical move: they continued improving the quality of the drug out on the street, so as to pull in even more customers.

Bari recalled: 'The old British gangsters didn't get it – they'd been selling shit cocaine for years and getting away with it. They not even noticing it was impacting on sales. That was fuckin' stupid of them because it helped give us even more business.

'As [a] result, we the Albanians became invincible. We took over cocaine trade in this country.'

Some criminologists have since hailed Albanian gangsters as 'criminal geniuses'. But to get this system to work, they've had to toil for years to gain control and influence in the major European and British ports, including Tilbury – just around the corner from The Crossing.

Today, the Albanians and their associates travel over The Crossing many times a week to monitor their 'goods', which often initially turn up at ports such as Rotterdam in Holland and are then put on vessels heading for Tilbury and other ports on the south-east coast of England, including Harwich.

In recent times British law enforcement has tried to step up its efforts to crack down on the Albanian Mafia by clamping down on Albanian criminals on the streets of London.

One Albanian cocaine baron was arrested in 2017 at a London petrol station with false Italian identification documents on his car and two kilos of the drug hidden in the boot. He was later given a heavy jail sentence.

'But those convictions are few and far between,' said old-school Kent gangster Pat King. 'I heard that sometimes the Albanians are prepared to sacrifice their own men to the cozzers [police] just to make the police feel less desperate about losing their war with the drug barons.'

Another British old-school gangster from Essex explained: 'It's rare for any Albanians to get arrested. And a lot of this is down to their ability to avoid tit-for-tat feuds with their rivals, so no one is prepared to inform on them.'

Albanian drug baron Bari explained: 'Most Albanians working here are charming, good-looking guys, but we will kill you if you cross us.' However, he insisted that his fellow countrymen are much less aggressive than is often portrayed in the media: 'We're sophisticated, professional and we do what we promise: we always deliver.'

Many Eastern European gangs in the UK also moved in on the protection rackets market in London and south-east England. Again, this is something that used to be the exclusive domain of homegrown English gangsters.

Many of the shipping containers and a few warehouses used by the Albanians for their criminal activities near The Crossing were allegedly 'given to them' by British criminals, who didn't have enough cash to pay off their debts to the Albanians. So, while Albanians, Bulgarians and Romanians stepped up their invasion of the territories in and around The Crossing itself, other Eastern European gangsters became just as active in the rest of the UK. And all of them used The Crossing to travel to and from their home countries on a regular basis.

Take the Polish. Unlike the other Eastern Europeans, they have had a presence in the UK for much longer, thanks to the close history between the UK and Poland that goes back to the Second World War.

The Poles' two main centres of population have for many years been the county of Lincolnshire and large chunks of West London, although they have a presence in many other communities across the UK as well.

West London provided the Poles with the most opportunities and their high arrest record in the UK is ample evidence of their illicit activities. In 2016, for example, nearly 35,000 Polish citizens were arrested here. Undoubtedly, many of those arrested are Polish gangsters, who are renowned for violence.

Andrzej Kulesza, twenty-seven, was beaten for three days before his body was dumped in a Northampton field by other Polish gangsters. A ligature was found around his neck. Minutes earlier, he'd texted his girlfriend, pleading with her to pay his captors: 'I'm begging you,' he said. She paid, but the gang wanted more and when that sum was not forthcoming, they decided to murder him.

Earlier, a group of men had forced their way into the home of a friend of Andrzej's and tortured him with a bicycle lock, knocking out two teeth, and threatened him with a knife to reveal where Andrzej was.

The friend's mobile phone was stolen and used to call two more associates of Andrzej in the hunt for him. That same stolen phone was then used to text Andrzej – and it drew him out of his home in Stamford Hill, Hackney, where he was snatched by armed men.

Andrzej was involved in dealing drugs – cannabis and amphetamines – and was in debt to Misiak so he had reason to fear for his safety. He was later reported missing to Tottenham police by his girlfriend – he had said he was going out to buy milk and bread at the local shop, but never returned home.

Andrzej's girlfriend grew increasingly concerned and started calling friends and acquaintances. She was eventually told he had been kidnapped and she would need to pay a ransom.

She was then contacted by Andrzej himself, who pleaded with her to help him and provide cash. He was crying and screaming and said his kidnappers were threatening to kill him. He said he was ordered to do press-ups and when he couldn't, he was beaten again and again.

Andrzej's girlfriend borrowed £300 from a friend and handed over the cash to another man at a rendezvous point off the North Circular at Edmonton. Promises were made that Andrzej would be released. Then another £500 was demanded but the calls then ended abruptly.

A member of the public walking her dog found Andrzej's remains in a field near Northampton, many months later. The skeleton was eventually pieced together and DNA tests proved it was Andrzej's.

The prime suspect for the murder was Polish gang boss Grzegorz Misiak, who later died in a mystery car crash.

Then there was Kamil Dreszer, twenty-seven, a Pole who had settled in Enfield, North London. After being found guilty of murder, kidnapping, false imprisonment and preventing the lawful burial and disposal of a corpse, he was jailed for life with a minimum of twenty-two years.

Dreszer's associate Artur Janik, aged twenty-six, of Walsall, West Midlands, was sentenced to fourteen years for similar charges. Another gang member – Daniel Kosowski, forty, of Beckton, East London, was jailed for thirty months for preventing a lawful burial.

Investigating officer Detective Chief Inspector Andy Chalmers from the Homicide and Serious Crime Command said: 'The three defendants, seeking revenge for a debt, kidnapped and tortured the victim before dumping his body in a remote location, presumably imagining it would never be found.'

Polish gangsters often tend to sidestep more traditional underworld sources of income such as drugs and prostitution to carry out more old-fashioned crimes such as robbery, which often involve much more use of violence.

One gang of Polish robbers were jailed in the UK for stripping, beating and smothering a self-made millionaire to death because they wanted his £20,000 Rolex watch. The gang had identified the man as a target after a Polish man who had supplied the victim with escort girls revealed he was wealthy.

The wealthy businessman was found dead at his £850,000 luxury home in Potters Bar, Hertfordshire, on 22 October 2014. He had been smothered with a pillow before his naked body was trussed up and covered with foam stuffing from a sofa. His body was discovered after his business manager raised the alarm, a court later heard.

The only item that police could confirm was missing was the Rolex, although it is thought the robbers may have been looking for hidden cash when they tore apart the sofa.

Three Polish gangsters based in the UK were eventually arrested and brought to trial for the murder. They were sentenced to more than fifty years' imprisonment between them at the Old Bailey.

The judge at their trial later said the victim had been a 'troubled soul' in the last few years of his life. He also told the court the robbery had taken 'extensive planning' and there had been great efforts after the man's death to remove all traces that might lead back to the killers, including disinfecting the property.

UK police and border control agents openly admit it is just too easy for many foreign criminals to slip in and out of the UK. Take Polish gangster Mariusz Florowski, who was wanted for a string of gang offences in his homeland but managed to slip into Britain in 2012. This much-feared gangster was left free to roam the UK, even boasting about the kidnappings he had carried out for the Warsaw Mafia.

Soon after arriving in the UK, Florowski had tortured another criminal – Benedykt Nowak, thirty-four – and then roasted his face with a blow torch before dousing him in petrol after the garage owner refused to hand over his business.

Florowski – said in court to be a fully paid-up member of the Warsaw Mafia – had already teamed up with mini cab firm boss Jakub Ostrowski, thirty-seven, who also had a string of convictions in Poland for attacking police officers.

Ostrowski had been running a cab firm called Polish Airbus, ferrying Polish immigrants to and from airports, after he arrived in Britain. The court heard that the pair wanted to use Nowak's garage to service Ostrowski's vehicles and had pestered Nowak and his brother for months before they decided to force them to hand over garage space.

The two gangsters then turned up at the premises at Dilloway Industrial Estate, in Southall, West London, and drank four bottles of vodka with the two Nowak brothers, who were also Polish. They then launched a brutal onslaught, kicking Pzemyslan all over his body. He ran and hid under a car, but was dragged back in to witness the horrific attack on his brother.

When Benedykt begged them not to kill his brother, Florowski turned a blow torch on his face, causing horrific injuries to his head and neck. Then both brothers were doused in petrol as Florowski walked between them, continually flicking the blow-torch ignition.

The victim's brother, Pzemyslan, twenty-six, was then forced to watch in terror as Florowski set Nowak alight, sending flames roaring up to the ceiling of the warehouse. He then snarled at Pzemyslan: 'I'm going to finish you as well,' before setting his brother Benedykt alight. He then fled in a Mercedes.

Horrific images were captured on CCTV of the victim staggering from the garage as flames burnt every scrap of clothing from his body. The fireball also caused tanks and cylinders to explode and the resulting blaze threatened to engulf neighbouring homes and businesses. Residents had to be evacuated as the fire spread further to a church, although no one else was hurt.

Nowak – who had only become a father a month earlier – was rushed to hospital but died of his injuries two days later.

The Old Bailey later heard how Florowski was wanted in Poland for a catalogue of gang-related offences yet he was able to sneak into Britain undetected in the middle of 2012 because the authorities had failed to issue a European Arrest Warrant. He had an appalling record of violence back in Poland, with convictions for armed robbery, firearms, extortion, burglary, possession of a firearm, as well as organised criminal gang activity.

The victim's devastated brother Pzemyslan told the court: 'I feel guilty that my brother died and I survived. I feel a great emptiness in my life. My best friend and my brother is gone.'

Florowski grinned as he and Ostrowski were jailed for life and ordered to serve at least thirty years each for murder and attempted murder.

Judge Rebecca Poulet told the unrepentant gangster: 'This attack involved sadistic conduct and almost unimaginable cruelty. In my view, your failure to get your way with the Nowak brothers is part of the reason for your wicked and cruel behaviour.'

The Polish authorities later announced they intended to put Florowski on trial in Poland for gang offences after he had served his UK prison sentence.

* * *

High-profile arrests of Eastern European criminals in the UK are seen as nothing more than the tip of the iceberg when it comes to the vast number of foreign gangsters who have immersed themselves in communities in Kent and Essex close to The Crossing. Occasionally, these criminals even inform on their associates to ensure they are 'removed' from the underworld. One such example was Bulgarian ganglord Tihomir Georgiev, forty-three. He was suspected of several atrocities – including a number of brutal murders – when arrested by Scotland Yard, who raided a London gym back in 2012.

Georgiev was on Interpol's list of Europe's most-wanted criminals. He had fled Bulgaria to escape trial, but was tracked down by investigative journalists from the *Sun* newspaper in London, who had then alerted the police.

Known as Tisho the Boxer, Georgiev was renowned for slicing off the ears and fingers of his victims. He had at one time been a henchman for notorious Bulgarian Mafia leader Zlatomir Ivanov, who controlled a vast empire of drugs, prostitution and money laundering and, in 2012, aspired to spread his criminal organisation to the UK.

After reaching London, his representative Georgiev was said to have lived rough on the streets of the capital before gym owner John Rooney Jnr gave him a room to live and allowed him to use the gym, unaware of his murky past.

* * *

Meanwhile, there remains one self-contained corner of the British underworld which no foreign criminals would dare enter. The city of Liverpool is still run by old-school British gangsters, who have effectively sealed off the entire community to foreign gangs.

Veteran Liverpool criminal Tommy Boy explained: 'It's a credit to us scousers that not even the Eastern Europeans had the bottle to try and take us on.'

Liverpool consolidated itself as the independent crime capital of Britain mainly thanks to its port facilities, which enabled local gangsters to buy drugs direct from the cartels in South America.

Tommy Boy recalled: 'I do remember a couple of Eastern European gangsters turning up here, a few years back. They asked for a meetin' in a local hotel – I think they was after our shipping route from South America because of the port. But we didn't turn up for the meeting and they scarpered.

'You gotta realise this place is a law unto itself. We had spotters on every street corner in places like Toxteth before many of those foreign gangsters were even born.

'We've always cut out all the middlemen, so no one could lean on us. We run things from the moment anything arrives on dry land.'

Even foreign gangsters like Albanian drug lord Bari admitted there were no plans to target Liverpool: 'It's not worth it. Liverpool is not somewhere any of us would want to invade.

We leave it to Scousers, but I bet someone will one day take them on and destroy them.'

* * *

So why and how has an entire subterranean underworld emerged in such close proximity to The Crossing, which is run almost entirely by Eastern European gangsters?

Bari explained: 'The Crossing was vital for our "businesses" so it made sense to move into the area. In many ways, it reminds us of our home countries. Rundown industrial estates. Dirty streets. Few people around. Almost deserted. It is an ideal environment for us.'

Besides the car number plate one-stop shop, there are numerous other shipping containers used by foreign criminals as storage facilities, flop houses for gangsters on the run and even a money exchange shop where Eastern European gangsters can swap their local currency for pounds. But the reason why local law enforcement has failed to break up this shady underworld is because the majority of these so-called 'facilities' are in shipping containers that can be moved around at a moment's notice on the backs of lorries.

Bari explained: 'We can move the containers round any time we want. It's [the] perfect system because by [the] time anyone knows we [are] in an area, we [are] gone.'

The insides of many of these containers are specially constructed and fitted out in a small factory, fifty miles from the Albanian capital of Tirana. In many cases, they even have their own hook-on power and water supplies.

'They [are] well equipped, but you would never know what was inside them because they look like dirty, rusty containers from outside,' said Bari. 'We are professionals in everything we do. We need to use these containers in [the] UK to make sure no one closes us down like they would do if we used just normal properties. This way we operate without the police knowing.

'We keep many special containers near to The Crossing so that our boys can use them after they drive through Europe, cross [the] Channel and get here often without ever having to stop, except for fuel. This is important to avoid many electronic surveillance systems operated by police in Europe. And of course we also switch number plates at least three times between here and Albania to make sure there is no actual record of our movements.'

One retired Kent detective noted: 'The Eastern Europeans always keep their men and their businesses very fluid, so it's harder to track down what they are up to. We've heard rumours about containers being converted into all sorts of things but we've never managed to actually find them.'

Sometimes, though, even the Eastern European gangs cannot resist letting the old-school criminals and the police know that they are the top dogs.

4

THE TUNNEL BOYS

One of the most-feared Eastern European gangs operating in the UK is led by a Romanian orphan brought up in the tunnels beneath Bucharest – home to hundreds of men, women and children, often stricken by drug abuse HIV and TB.

When Romania's last communist leader Nicolae Ceausescu died in 1989 there were tens of thousands of children in orphanages and in state 'care' in Romania. There were scenes of such neglect and cruelty that many closely resembled the concentration camps of the last war. Eventually, many of these orphans escaped, went on the run and ended up in the maze of sewage tunnels beneath the Romanian capital, just as alone but at least free from their cruel captors.

Amongst them a decade ago was a little boy, Dragos, who looked about ten when he was in fact fourteen. Dragos eventually emerged from the tunnels with a gang of other orphans and together they formed a notorious street gang in Bucharest: The Tunnel Boys. But when police finally tried to crack down on the gang, they dispersed and Dragos and some of his associates were smuggled into the UK on false passports.

Today, Dragos is the gangmeister behind some of the most trigger-happy teenagers you are ever likely to meet. Some still call him 'Dragon' after his street-fighting days. He has a tattoo on his inner thigh, which reads: 'Dragon, King of the Sewers'. But these days Dragos lives near The Crossing and enjoys a life of luxury compared to those awful far-off days when he faced abuse on virtually a daily basis.

As leader of The Tunnel Boys, Dragos has encouraged many other abandoned Romanian orphans to come to the UK and join his gang. Other Eastern European gangs sometimes hire Dragos and his fearless band of 'soldiers' to humiliate their enemies, just as they did on Friday, 5 August 2018.

* * *

The enormous arches of the Queen Elizabeth II Bridge were majestically backlit by the sun dipping slowly down from the west as it burnt through a glittering haze rippling across the surface of the River Thames. This time on a Friday evening was usually rush hour for tens of thousands of motorists, but it was holiday season so the carriageway heading south was surprisingly quiet. However, those who did use The Crossing that night could not have failed to notice the slip-stream of four jet-skis surging westwards up the river at high speed.

Despite the warm weather, the pilots all wore wetsuits and goggles. They belonged to The Tunnel Boys gang.

'It's like the scooter boys wearing helmets. This means no one knows who they are, even if the police are watching,' explained Dragos.

The jet-skis had set out a few minutes earlier from the shore, a short distance from a scrapyard that the Tunnel Boys had just taken over within the shadow of The Crossing.

'They'd had their eyes on that yard for ages because it has a furnace,' explained local criminal Ginger. 'I heard they use the furnace to melt down all the old mobile phones cos they go through them at a rate of ten a week.'

The yard had belonged for more than three decades to a once notorious old-school Kent biker gang of criminals but they'd had to hand it over to the Eastern Europeans after a shipment of drugs had been lost in transit by the Brits, who had broken their own golden rule and agreed to work for the 'foreigners'.

Kent criminal Albert explained: 'We'd pretty much lost the war against the foreigners by this time, so had to go cap in hand to them for a few scraps of work. But working for the Eastern Europeans nearly always ends in tears. We all found ourselves working under different rules and their rules are pretty fuckin' hard.'

Only a few months before those jet-skis had set out upriver, two Bulgarian gangsters based in Kent had disappeared after a shipment of cocaine was lost on board a yacht as it sailed from southern France to Ramsgate, on the Kent coast. Some local gangsters believe the Bulgarians may well have ended up in the furnace at the scrapyard now run by The Tunnel Boys and used to destroy all trace of everything, from laptops to body parts.

Meanwhile, the jet-skis continued their journey defiantly under the Queen Elizabeth II Bridge and west in the direction of London. It was another statement from the Eastern

Europeans to the British gangsters to leave them to run things from now on.

The Tunnel Boys leader Dragos later explained: 'Every now and again the British gangsters try to win back territory near The Crossing and they must be shown who is running things.'

The four jet-skis' trip upriver that evening took them past many iconic landmarks connected to the history of the underworld when the British were still 'the guv'nors'. Much of the old docklands on the north and south banks of the Thames had been occupied by criminal gangs going all the way back to the 1800s and many of today's so-called old school British gangsters came from families whose involvement with crime had been fed by the river, often going back three or four generations.

'But that didn't mean anything when the foreign gangs took us apart,' said Albert. 'The river was the key to the underworld back in the old days. Everything went in and out of the docks that existed right in the centre of London in those days. Back then, crime thrived and a lot of us wish it was all as simple as that now, but it ain't.'

At one stage, those four jet skis surged at speed past a pub on the south riverbank near Bermondsey in the London borough of Southwark, where many old-school British gangsters still drink.

'That was like a further insult to the old Brits: we were telling them we could do what the fuck we wanted,' Dragos explained. 'The war's over, so they have nothing to fight about anymore.'

To many homegrown gangsters the 'river run' by the Romanian gangsters on jet-skis must have felt like another nail in their coffin. And as those lightweight vessels skimmed along the river on that warm summer's evening, it seemed the police were also on holiday because no one was even attempting to intercept the vessels as they continued speeding up the river.

* * *

The river police are a uniquely skilled band of officers who work entirely separately from the rest of the police in London, Essex and Kent. Their history closely mirrors the development of crime on water, especially in the areas dominated by The Crossing.

The Thames Marine Police were formed in 1798 to supposedly cooperate with other security and crime prevention organisations. This included all types of work connected to crime and accidents, from the terror attacks to everyday suicides, and from the major shipping disasters to the crises around political refugees.

A few years before those jet-skis powered their way up the Thames, Essex and Kent police forces had agreed to work much more closely together, following acknowledgement that foreign gangsters had been taking over a lot of territory in Kent and Essex.

Under this unofficial new partnership, the two forces also teamed up on policing The Crossing, as well as ports and airports on both sides of the River Thames. Kent Police were even given use of Essex's police helicopter.

* * *

Back on the river that August evening, those four machines piloted by the cocky Tunnel Boys eventually reached Canary Wharf on the edge of the City of London. It was only then that a police boat finally set off from a quay and started powering in their direction.

Canary Wharf is another significant location when it comes to British criminal history because its development into one of the world's foremost financial business centres is in part due to the proceeds from the Brink's-Mat gold bullion robbery, back in 1983. That legendary crime was committed by some of the very same gangsters now clashing with these foreign 'invaders'.

Three of the Brink's-Mat gang invested money from their stolen gold in property on the Canary Wharf site when it consisted of wasteland and crumbling, abandoned Victorian warehouses. They sold off the land at vast profit to developers, who then created the tower blocks now housing many of the world's biggest banks.

Out on the river that night, The Tunnel Boys didn't panic when they saw the police boat surging towards them. They simply pirouetted around and headed at high speed back east towards The Crossing. When another police boat joined the chase, The Tunnel Boys increased their speed until they were far enough ahead to land their machines on the riverbank, hoist them onto waiting trailers and make their escape in a convoy of SUVs before any police cars could even find their location.

'I know the boys who were on the jet-skis and I can tell you, they enjoyed every moment of that,' Romanian gangster Sami later revealed.

Former armed robber Geoff, from Bermondsey, told me: 'Yeah, those lads on the jet-skis were outrageous! They'd worked out they could outrun the police and so they went for it.

'In some ways I have to admit it was classy but if you look at it in the cold light of day, they were taking the piss out of us and the cozzers all in one night.'

The sheer nerve of that jet-ski 'stunt' by The Tunnel Boys undoubtedly further humiliated many British gangsters much more than they've ever cared to admit.

Around this time, many older British villains began arriving back from recession-hit Spain, having run out of cash. Most of them knew the foreign gangs had taken over, but, in desperation, they decided to launch an offensive to try and steal back The Crossing.

* * *

Just after Christmas 2018, a gang of old-school criminals fire-bombed the headquarters – a shipping container, naturally – of a gang of friendly, polite Romanian car washers just a short stone's throw from The Crossing.

Locals were so upset they had a whip-round to collect enough money for the Romanians to be able to afford to buy another shipping container to place in the corner of the car park where they operated, just overlooking the Thames Estuary. At the time, one of the Romanians – he called himself Ken – insisted he and his fellow workers had no direct connections to the Eastern European gangs now running the area.

'We are independent,' he told one local newspaper reporter. 'Some of the British think we have links to the Romanian gangsters who live round here but that is not true. We are just hard-working guys trying to make an honest living. You know what I mean?'

Whatever the truth of the matter, the arson attack on the Romanians was yet another reminder of how much bitterness still existed between the local old-school criminals and their foreign rivals.

One Kent armed robber called Benny insisted the car wash was owned by the Romanian Mafia: 'Listen, it had to go. We've taken enough shit off them in the last few years. This was our way of telling the foreign gangs to back off.'

It was also clear that this sort of attack was to increase as tensions worsened between the long-term enemies. Ultimately, few people believed the British criminals would ever mount a successful comeback: 'They already fucked,' said Albanian criminal Bari. 'So why burn down a little car wash? They not learn their lesson?'

Ironically, the attack on the Romanian car washers united the locals against many of the British old-school criminals, who had plagued the area for the past fifty years.

'Those boys were nice to have around,' said one local resident. 'They was polite and extremely good at their jobs. Those old-fashioned British gangsters should never have done what they did.'

Old-school Kent criminal Ned even concurred: 'They sneaked in after the car washing blokes had left for the evening and torched the container. It was pathetic! Those Romanian guys hadn't hurt a fly.

'No doubt the old-time villains was trying to show the Eastern Europeans they was not dead and buried. But it didn't work because even the local residents ended up slagging the old-school villains off. Many locals construed the attack as being racially motivated and maybe they were right.'

To be fair, some residents were not so pro the Romanians.

'I'm fuckin' angry about the foreign gangs but there's no point in taking it out on a bunch of poorly paid car washers –

they're not the evil criminals who are causing all the trouble,' said one.

Whatever the truth behind this arson attack, the Romanians were back operating their car washing business fully within a few days of the raid. The old-school British gangsters – many of whom had just arrived back from Spain with venom in their veins – then discovered just how powerful the Eastern Europeans could be.

A few days after the attack on the car wash, three Fiat Pandas turned up at a pub near Dartford, Kent, which was popular with old-school gangsters. Eight men of Eastern European appearance burst into the pub, held all the customers at gunpoint, stole money from the till and pistol-whipped two men known to have been involved in the car wash attack.

The old-school criminals were left stunned that the foreign gangsters would dare to come onto their 'territory' in such a brazen manner. No one reported the raid to the police because these characters simply never involve the long arm of the law in any of their disputes. But those British criminals – including the ones just back from Spain – soon retreated back into the shadows.

Indeed, many British gangsters – especially in Kent and Essex – found themselves with no choice but to carry out crimes they never thought they'd have to stoop to. Some even began touting for business as people smugglers.

'That was a desperate sign,' said local gangster Ned. 'They were really stooping that low to try and make a living. It showed the foreign gangs just how useless we all were.'

One British gang is known to have carried out a successful trip in a rigid-hulled inflatable boat (RHIB) called *Rebel*, later found abandoned on the beach at Dymchurch, on the Kent coast, with children's life jackets on board on 11 May 2016.

When border officials went to investigate, the professed owner claimed to have been out 'night fishing' when he experienced engine trouble.

Two weeks later, French police spotted another group of people signalling a boat called the *Antares* RHIB in the water off Cran d'Escalles beach, near Calais.

A group of migrants waded out to meet it. The vessel was due to pick up eighteen migrants, including two children aged sixteen and seventeen and a woman, but it suddenly left before they reached it after a parked car signalled, using its headlights as a warning.

Two days later, the same gang tried again with a newly acquired vessel called *White Scanner* RHIB, but this time the boat ran out of fuel and the migrants were forced to start bailing out as it flooded with seawater. The terrified group of refugees sent desperate text messages, with one saying: 'We are in England, tell police, we are drowning.'

Coastguard helicopter and RNLI crews were eventually able to rescue those stranded onboard and two British criminals were arrested and later each jailed for four years. Immigration officials said the Albanian victims were 'in a perilous state' and facing potential death when they were rescued.

Another gang of British criminals bought a larger boat from Southampton, which they referred to as *The Boat With No Name*. But they didn't realise that National Crime Agency (NCA) operatives had planted a bug on the boat to listen in as the gang plotted a people smuggling migrant run.

One member of the gang took the *Boat With No Name* out to pick up some refugees but ran into rough sea and turned back. Eventually, they had to be rescued by NCA officers shadowing them. They had contingency plans to try and run the migrants across the world's busiest shipping route on jet-skis but, luckily, they never got the chance.

'Fuckin' amateurs!' declared Albanian criminal Bari. 'It's [a] good thing they get arrested because those refugees might have died if they [were] left floating in middle of sea.'

A Kent court was later told that the migrants, including men, women and children, had been charged up to £6,000 each to journey across the English Channel. The British gang had little boating experience and were apparently ignorant of the dangers they were exposing their victims to. In fact, it later emerged that the same gang had even made several earlier unsuccessful attempts to transport migrants across the Channel in other lightweight crafts.

The NCA secretly filmed those old-school gangsters meeting with their Albanian 'business partners' in a pub car park. They moved in to arrest them amid safety fears that they might decide to use the jet-skis. Six Britons ended up being jailed.

'In some ways it was much more shaming for the British boys to be caught like that,' explained one-time Bermondsey bank robber Val.

'They'd tried to show the foreigners how to do it and found out it wasn't as easy as they thought.'

Gradually, British gangs – depleted by the foreign invasion – were discovering that people smuggling was not such an easy way to earn money.

In the summer of 2018, three more Kent criminals – two Brits and a Vietnamese – smuggled four Vietnamese men into the UK in a dinghy. They were also monitored and recorded by undercover police and later found guilty of people trafficking and sentenced to a total of more than thirty years in prison. It then emerged that four other members of the same gang – all from Albania – had facilitated the trip and even provided the refugees. The British gang members were jailed for their role in the operation.

Today, many old-school British gangsters suspect that Albanian gangsters deliberately informed police about their so-called crime partners – the British – to ensure that they were forced out of the people smuggling business. Kent criminal Albert explained: 'The Albanians led us into trap after trap. They knew we was desperate to make some cash, so they made out they was helping us by lining up the Albanian refugees. But then they let the police know what we was up to. Brits would never do that to other villains but the Eastern Europeans don't even understand what the word loyalty means.'

In another completely separate case, a British criminal was jailed after seventeen Albanians arrived in his boat at Chichester marina, in Sussex. Each had paid 6,000 euros (£5,000) to make the trip across the Channel.

One police investigator later said: 'Human beings were being treated as a commodity, as cargo. They were not provided with life jackets, just brought across the busiest shipping lanes in the world, at night.'

Prosecutor Wayne Cleaver told the jury some migrants were 'so desperate' for asylum, they were 'prepared to undertake such a treacherous journey': 'They seldom do so without the connivance of criminal gangs, whose primary interest is financial profit rather than any more noble motive.'

The migrants – who did not speak English – were only located after police, in a speculative move, stopped a van driven by one of the smugglers.

* * *

The gradual and successful takeover by foreign gangs of multiple territories in the UK has been going on for much longer than most old-school gangsters care to remember. Some believe that the Eastern Europeans have been operating with impunity for as long as fifteen years in some parts of Kent and Essex, including the area around The Crossing.

Back in 2007, just after that pivotal Tonbridge cash deposit heist, a gang of Eastern European criminals was already exploiting Britain's lax border controls to smuggle tens of thousands of economic migrants into the UK over the following years. Families were paying up to £14,000 per person to be taken from Turkey across Europe and into the UK by plane, train, lorry and ferry.

The gang was later said in a UK court to have masterminded operations in France, Belgium, Holland, Denmark, Austria and Italy as they smuggled people through twenty-one European countries and across the Channel. Indeed, the scale of the operation sparked a demand from politicians in the UK at the time for a tightening of border controls, but nothing much was done and gradually more and more foreign gangs started running their own people smuggling operations as the numbers of refugees flooding in from war-torn Middle East countries spiked over the following few years.

* * *

By 2018, it seems the remnants of the most powerful old-school gangs in London, Essex and Kent had disintegrated and foreign gangs were dominating the underworld, especially in those areas close to The Crossing.

'They were fuckin' everywhere!' sighed former bank robber Ned. 'Most of us couldn't move a muscle without them knowing all about it. We were trapped in our own shit!'

And by this time the Eastern European gangs were totally dominating the people smuggling businesses on the south coasts of Kent and East Sussex. This was proven beyond doubt when, in November 2018, two Albanian men transported illegal immigrants across the English Channel in a flimsy, over-loaded inflatable vessel. Their passengers had no life vests or navigation equipment and sailed across a busy shipping lane in total darkness.

Experts later said that attempting to cross the Channel in a boat that size was like trying to cross the M25 at its busiest time on foot – they even used empty water bottles for bailing water out of the boat.

Feim Vata, thirty-two, and Xhemal Baco, twenty-four, were arrested after picking up those six Albanians in France and bringing them ashore near Deal, in Kent. They were believed to have made the trip at night at least three times previously.

Vata and Baco – who both lived in Buckinghamshire – were each jailed for eight years at Canterbury Crown Court after admitting conspiracy to assist unlawful immigration. But the relatively small number of arrests for such offences continues to indicate that the majority of people smuggling operations still go unchecked by the British authorities.

Meanwhile, bitter and twisted old-school criminals were festering as they served out long prison sentences which had begun before the foreign gangs even surged through the badlands of Essex and Kent. By this time, virtually all British gangsters had stepped back from the territories around The Crossing, especially since that fire-bombing on the Romanian car washers by those gangsters just back from Spain. But the British jailbirds refused to accept that the Eastern Europeans were now in charge – even from their 'impotent' prison cells.

Then one of Britain's most notorious professional criminals – we'll call him Lou – was let out of prison on day release. He immediately headed for his old stomping grounds of Dartford and Swanley, both very near to The Crossing and in the heart of the notorious area of Kent known as 'The Bermuda Triangle'.

One of Lou's oldest associates – Pat – later explained: 'Lou was determined to get back what he believed was his. He'd been stuck in prison for years, always claiming he'd been framed for a murder by a bunch of crooked cops and most of us believed him.

'Now he was out and he couldn't accept that he was no longer the top dog in those towns around The Crossing.'

Initially, crime boss Lou had to tread carefully and keep a low profile because he was on day release and didn't want to get sent back to prison to serve the remainder of his sentence.

'So, Lou quietly carried out a low-key tour of all his old haunts to try and get some of his old mates fired up,' explained Pat.

Here, Kent old-school professional robber Albert takes up the story: 'Behind the scenes, Lou was trying to get a load of old-timers together to mount an operation to take back The Crossing and all the territory around it.

'It was madness. Nearly twenty years had passed since Lou was banged up and here he was, acting as if nothing had changed.

'He just didn't realise how powerful the foreign gangs had become.'

Naturally, it wasn't too long before Eastern European gangsters operating in and around The Crossing heard about Lou's plans.

'The foreign gangsters warned off all the younger local criminals that anyone who helped Lou would be putting their own lives at risk,' Albert explained. 'But there were some old-timers egging Lou on because they were still bitter about the foreigners. They just didn't seem to realise they were completely out-numbered in every sense of the word.'

For a few weeks – following Lou's release from prison – there was a stand-off between warring factors. Albert later explained: 'The foreigners encouraged all the rest of us to talk to Lou and make him see sense. They could have just stepped in and done Lou there and then, but they respected the fact Lou had once been a big face and they wanted a peaceful conclusion.'

But Lou – the once all-powerful British crime boss – did not fully appreciate his perilous position, it seems.

Albert explained: 'The Albanians heard that Lou and some of his oldest mates had got themselves tooled up [armed] through a local gun dealer, which meant Lou was deadly serious.'

Then, a few days later, two of Lou's closest associates disappeared.

'The Eastern Europeans were sending out a message to Lou and his lads,' Albert continued. 'But Lou refused to be intimidated. He made sure the Albanians heard that he was still after their blood. He was deliberately trying to wind them up, it was fuckin' madness. But Lou said he didn't have anything to lose.'

Within hours, Lou was being closely shadowed on the streets of Dartford by three men in a black Fiat 500. He'd just left a pub where he'd met up with another old-school Essex crime boss.

'They'd been talkin' about how to beat the Albanians,' said Albert.

Lou was never seen again.

Albert explained: 'Lou disappeared into thin air. Maybe he decided to hotfoot it before they got him, or maybe they just did him in.'

As word of Lou's disappearance spread across Kent and Essex, at least half a dozen associates of the 'missing' crime boss sold up their detached homes and moved abroad at short notice.

'That was a bad loss for all of us,' recalled Albert. 'Lou thought he was going to be our saviour, but he should have kept his trap shut and gone into retirement in the sunshine. He had stacks of cash from his previous "jobs" before he got banged up, but he couldn't stand not being the boss when he got out of prison.

'The Eastern Europeans used Lou as a warning to others. And even though we don't really know what happened to him, it worked. Most of the Brits who still wanted a ruck with the foreigners got the message and stepped back.'

Lou's disappearance undoubtedly helped the Eastern European gangs based in and around The Crossing to further consolidate their powerbase in the area.

Drug lord Bari explained: 'We are experts at scaring people so they not hurt us. That guy Lou was stupid old man living in the past.'

Most Eastern European gangsters insist that killing their enemies is definitely a last resort but they do often use chilling 'associates' to scare their foes into submission.

Bari explained: 'The key to our success is to make others afraid of us so we Albanians have "secret weapon" – special man who come back and forth between here and Albania. Here, he often stays for few weeks in one of our converted containers.'

That 'secret weapon' is a suspected serial killer called Driza, wanted by police in Albania for a number of murders.

'Driza is one of scariest motherfuckers you ever meet,' said Bari. 'This guy come here first time from Albania to escape police. Now, he goes back to Albania whenever he want.'

Driza first arrived in the UK in 2016, as a lorry driver, but, according to Bari, the Albanian Mafia then recruited him as a henchman and made sure everyone knew about the serial killings he'd been linked to, back in Albania.

'We like to strike fear into our enemies so we don't have to use our guns to keep them behaving good,' he explained. 'Driza is perfect for scaring shit out of Brits.'

Bari also claims that Driza often works as a torturer for the Albanian Mafia in the UK: 'We protect him from the police back in Albania now, but he work for us in exchange. It's good deal for all of us.'

* * *

Having seemingly won the war with the old-school British gangsters, the mainly Eastern European gangs in the UK even created specific 'strategies' to infiltrate new potentially lucrative targets for robberies and other crimes.

Bari explained: 'Foreign gangsters here have many of their men in jobs in cash security businesses throughout UK. They can then target good places for robberies, like they did with Tonbridge heist.'

With Eastern European gangs using The Crossing as a transport hub into Kent, Essex and many parts of London, they've also been extremely skilled at setting up safe houses in specific communities where they can keep a low profile and take some much-needed rest before committing more crimes.

One classic example of this is in the Essex coastal town of Westcliff-on-Sea. Bari said: 'We have three houses in town where our men are based. They send out dealers in cars, scooters and on bicycles, day and night. It's perfect place for us.'

Eastern European gangs are ultra-cautious about CCTV cameras and other forms of surveillance. Bari explained: 'Many old-school Brits don't even realise that, these days, you being watched everywhere you go. That means not meeting customers or other gangsters in places where transaction might be seen and picture taken. This is obvious but many criminals don't think about this kind of stuff and then they end up in jail.'

At the main marina, next to the East Sussex seaside town of Eastbourne, one Eastern European gang is alleged to have set up a major drugs distribution centre inside a rented apartment, just a short distance from the marina itself.

Bari explained: 'Places like Westcliff and Eastbourne perfect locations for these type of operations. We bring much coke over in yachts. Then we take it to safe house, cut it and bag it. Usually this takes some days, even weeks, because safe house is many miles from where coke comes in. But in towns like Westcliff and Eastbourne we do it all in houses close by, which saves time and money.

'We like to flood marketplace and sell all that product quickly. No criminal wants drug shipments hanging around, not earning money. You get stuff in, you sell quickly. That's the key to this fuckin' business.'

* * *

By taking over the territory near The Crossing and into the surrounding countryside of both Kent and Essex, the Eastern European gangs have managed to 'conquer' entire towns and villages which are now 'fed' through so-called County Lines drug supply networks. These now dominate Middle England.

Old-school British drug baron Den said: 'The Eastern Europeans don't care about getting their hands dirty by sending their guys in to sell drugs direct to entire communities. British gangsters would never do this themselves, they consider themselves above such things.'

Albanian gangster Bari explained: 'We had British guy working for us who lived in big house on edge of housing estate. He was middleman for us because he knew all the kids on estate – he'd once been their main drugs supplier himself.

'This guy – I call him James – helped us make the connections we needed to permanently operate from territories without problems from rival gangs. The British kids backed off from us because they heard about reputation of Eastern European gangsters. But, in the end, James got so greedy, we had him removed and now we run it all directly ourselves.'

Meanwhile, old-school robber Ned insisted that he and his British 'associates' did not give up their 'businesses' as easily as the foreign gangs claim.

'It would be wrong to make out we just crumbled, but we was overrun,' he explained. 'The foreign gangs had so many people working for them and they was so tightly knitted that we never knew what any of them would get up to next.'

But by this time many British gangsters *had* undoubtedly already given up the fight. Pockets of resistance still existed in some of the more rural areas near The Crossing but those criminals made fewer and fewer incursions into the foreign gangs' territory because they were so heavily outnumbered and outgunned.

* * *

Meanwhile, The Crossing continued to provide foreign criminals with a quick getaway back to Europe, as well as easy access to the whole of the UK. By 2016, increasing numbers of foreign gangsters were committing their crimes in the UK and then leaving immediately – often before anyone had even realised they were there in the first place.

A classic example was hitman Gorgi, a Ukrainian national who claims to have been contracted to kill at least four criminals in the UK. Gorgi was based in the South of France but admitted to one criminal source that his biggest and richest 'customers' nearly always came from the UK. And like so many of the new wave of foreign criminals who have invaded Britain in recent years, he always travels in and out of the country by road.

'Flying is a big risk for someone like me,' he explained. 'There are too many security checks at airports and I can't bring my weapon of choice in anyway, so it would have to be smuggled in by road or bought from a dealer here. I might as well drive here.'

Gorgi claims virtually all his UK-based targets have been in Kent and Essex, so The Crossing is an area with which he is very familiar: 'The Crossing is vital for someone like me because I need to get in and out of the UK quickly. I'm not worried about the registration of my car because I don't come here that often and I don't have criminal record, so there is no reason for me to be flagged up.'

Gorgi says that UK authorities have made it 'too easy' to come in and out of the country and that is why he prefers to carry out hits on UK soil more than anywhere else in Europe: 'The police don't stop you much here unless they have a very good reason. That means you can do your business without interference.

'The other great thing about the UK is that there are now so many citizens here from across the world that a guy like me just doesn't really stand out.'

* * *

One of the most outrageous crimes committed in the UK by predominantly Eastern European gangsters is carjacking. As

Albanian drug lord Bari explained: 'British kids have tried to do this for years, but they [are] amateurs compared to us.'

In recent years, foreign gangs of carjackers have specifically targeted elite sports cars, such as Porsches and Ferraris and top-of-the-range SUVs: 'They must be worth at least £100,000 for us to make big money,' said Bari.

Target vehicles are often followed after having tracking devices attached to them so that the gang can choose the perfect moment to pounce in quiet locations, preferably uncovered by CCTV cameras. These cars are then taken immediately to lorry parks – often near The Crossing – where the plates are swapped and then they are driven into shipping containers before being transported to Tilbury and Harwich or by road through Europe.

Often these stolen cars are shipped out to places like Northern Cyprus and then on to the Middle East, where there is a huge market for so-called prestige vehicles.

In recent years, Albanian gangs have been supplementing their personnel by 'specially importing' Kosovan nationals, who are considered the best carjackers of all.

Bari explained: 'Kosovans are madmen and they [are] fantastic drivers so this help us to strike even more fear into enemies.'

By early 2019, the number of daylight carjackings had increased dramatically in Kent and Essex compared to the previous couple of years. One classic example occurred in Essex in 2018 when a thirty-five-year-old man was dragged from his white sports car by armed, foreign-sounding gangsters after he stopped at traffic lights at a roundabout.

* * *

Eastern European gangsters have bedded in and around The Crossing so effectively that they have stepped up plans to sell increasing amounts of heroin on the streets of Britain. Thirty years ago, the drug was widely available in the UK but supplies have shrunk considerably in the past few years. London-based Turkish gangs were the market leaders, but a lot of their product ended up in other parts of Europe where heroin was taken by more people.

A few years back, a group of Albanian, Romanian and Bulgarian traffickers tried to set up a new supply route from Pakistan to bring bigger shipments of the drug into the UK. Some of these details were first uncovered when three UK-based Pakistani men were arrested and then prosecuted for heroin smuggling, back in 2013.

Mohammed Farooq, fifty-one, Homayon Mehrpoor, sixty-one, and Ahmad Shah, forty-four, were part of a conspiracy to smuggle heroin with a street value of £306 million – concealed in vegetables and bed linen – into the UK. The three men were given respective prison sentences of twenty-nine years, twenty-five years and twenty-nine years, while Farooq's wife, Catherine, fifty-five, was jailed for nine months for money laundering.

Farooq was ordered to repay £642,981 at Birmingham Crown Court after Canadian national Mehrpoor and Shah, from Pakistan, were earlier told to repay £346,519 and £389,018 respectively.

No doubt Eastern European gangsters then looked else-where for supplies of heroin to sell on the streets of Britain.

* * *

As has already been mentioned, Eastern Europe's most danger-ous criminals nearly always come from their homeland to the UK using false identities, which means authorities in this country have absolutely no idea who is on the streets of Britain at any one time.

Amongst those illegal 'visitors' to the UK are mother and daughter Monica and Kandra, who often travel in and out of this country from their home in Romania using different pass-ports each time. Once in the UK, they immediately get down to their business – contract killing – and then head back to Romania afterwards.

Monica, late-forties, and Kandra, mid-twenties, work for many Eastern European crime syndicates as freelance killers. They never meet the people who pay them to kill. Everything is done through at least two shadowy middlemen and this has no doubt helped them to avoid detection for some years.

Albanian drug lord Bari explained: 'Monica and Kandra two scary women. No one knows their real names. They very good at job because they blend in everywhere as mother and daughter. No one notices them.

'No one really knows anything more about them. They clever because that way, they not get caught.'

Not surprisingly, this extraordinary mother-and-daughter duo slip beneath the radar of most country's border controls. Often they will use disguises and few people even in their home country know about their real 'careers'.

'I hear they never look same,' explained Bari. 'They change hair, age, clothes, image … They brilliant and you would never know if they came looking for you until it was too late.'

It is rumoured in UK's foreign underworld circles that Monica and Kandra are not even really related but act like mother and daughter because it makes them appear less suspicious.

Bari explained: 'I was told they had husbands and children back home, but they keep this other side of their lives secret. Who knows if it is true or not?

'No one knows what UK murders they have carried out because they so good, you only would know if they have committed a murder if you ordered that job yourself.'

* * *

Back in the areas around The Crossing, memories of their crushing defeat at the hands of the foreign gangs in the badlands of Kent and Essex finally persuaded some old-school British criminals to agree to form a previously unheard of alliance in 2018.

Armed robber Sam explained: 'Kent and Essex villains finally came together. We recognised that unless we teamed up, we had no chance of taking those bastards on.'

But was it too little, too late?

As part of their plan to recapture territories in late 2018, the mainly all-white British gangs in Kent and Essex not only joined forces, but tried to recruit a gang of Yardies from Liverpool to help them take on the foreign gangs. It was well known that Liverpool was the only territory in the UK that the foreign gangs were afraid to try and 'invade.'

Yardie gangs consist mainly of men of Caribbean origin who specialised in drug smuggling and sales across many big cities in the UK, but in recent years they too have taken a hammering at the hands of the foreign criminals. Yardies based outside Liverpool had clashed with Eastern European gangs mainly in territories such as North and West London, where they once reigned supreme.

So, the Merseyside 'branch' of the Yardies was initially very receptive to the idea of joining forces with the old-school villains, despite a huge racial divide – which led to both camps being highly suspicious of each other's real motives.

'We told 'em, why not join forces with us and we'll go after the foreigners together,' explained Kent armed robber Keith. 'We knew a lot of the Eastern European gangsters hated black men and that they were really scared of the Liverpool gangs. Us and the Yardies seemed like the perfect combination.

'We'd been to many football matches abroad, where Eastern Europeans made monkey chants at black players and stuff like that, so we was convinced the Yardies would be up for it. But we soon realised it was a mistake when a couple of the Scouser Yardie bosses demanded we pay them out of our own pockets to be part of the team to take on the Eastern Europeans.'

Within days the Yardies 'experiment' crumbled when the English gangs from Kent and Essex began feuding with their so-called new 'business partners', the Liverpool Yardies.

'We fucked up badly on that one,' admitted Keith. 'The idea was to see off the Eastern Europeans but instead we ended up in a battle with the fuckin' Scouser Yardies, who accused us of being more racist than the foreign gangs.

'Maybe they had a point but this was all about getting the Eastern Europeans off our soil. We must have been a laughing stock when the foreign gangs found out what had happened to our plan.'

Drug lord Bari heard on the grapevine about the Yardie 'experiment' in Kent: 'Sure, many Eastern Europeans are racist, but these English gangsters are no better.

'When we heard about their plan, we just went in harder on the English gangs. Sure, these Yardies were from Liverpool, which we kept away from. But the British gangsters upset them anyway, so we never had that problem to deal with in the end – it didn't happen.'

* * *

Then there was Adrian 'The Dad' Botez, a Romanian inspired by the notorious 1990s Eastern European jewel thieves, The Pink Panthers.

Over a ten-year period, the Panthers had pulled off some of the most daring jewellery robberies of all time in cities including Cannes, Rome and Paris during which they got away with tens of millions of pounds worth of gems. The gang mostly consisted of former Serbian soldiers but few members of the Panthers were ever actually brought to justice during their heyday.

'The Dad' Botez ran a gang of similar 'ninja-like' jewel raiders, who had stolen £3.1 million worth of goods from eleven high-end stores across England in a one-year spree. In 2017, it emerged that the gang was taught everything they knew in a specially set up 'thieves academy' in Bucharest, Romania. Many of the 'students' were recruited from Botez's home town of Piatra Neamt in Eastern Romania. From there, new academy recruits were blindfolded and usually hidden in the boots of cars and then taken to the capital, Bucharest, for training.

The crime academy in Romania first opened after several gangs from the same region of the country employed similar strategies during raids and it was decided to 'pool' that talent.

One student who attended the academy in Bucharest later recalled it was organised like a military training school and included strict rules and rigorous training sessions.

'It was like a boot camp for criminals,' he explained. 'But what I learned there was invaluable.'

The UK raids connected to the academy students nearly all took place in shopping centres across the country and each one took the criminal gang less than ninety seconds. Initially, they would force entry into the mall itself, usually by smashing their way through glass front doors. They would then set a fire behind them as they went in – to prevent people following in after them.

Once inside their target stores they would smash the glass cabinets and steal only the most valuable objects. Some of the gang even cycled to the scene of their crime to avoid attracting attention. They also cordoned off sections of road to reduce traffic and observers. All of this had been taught to them at that academy back in Romania.

Sometimes the gangs would pitch tents two to three miles from the scene of their intended crime, even burying their own personal waste in a bid to avoid DNA being gathered later by police.

The gang behind these break-ins in the UK were only eventually caught by police thanks to an informant – a British gangster having an affair with one of the wives of the Eastern European robbers.

Six members of the gang were jailed for forty-seven years for offences, including one so-called bonanza raid, which netted them nearly £700,000 worth of cash and jewellery.

The Bucharest 'academy' was subsequently closed down by authorities in Romania. But it was then reopened close to The Crossing by a gang of Albanians and Romanians determined to train up their own handpicked rookie youngsters for further raids. They even purchased the 'rights' to the academy from original founder 'The Dad' Botez.

Romanian criminal Kira explained: 'It was easier to run our academy here in the UK than back in Romania. We attracted "students" mainly from other Eastern European countries who wanted to "work" here full time.'

The academy was run for some time from two shipping containers converted into 'classrooms' which travelled around Kent and Essex on the backs of lorries in much the same way as a mobile library does. Dozens of Eastern European and other foreign 'student' criminals are said to have attended the academy after it opened in the UK. Classes even included specialist training on how to spot valuable jewellery and gold at a glance.

Each member of these specially trained networks of robbers was also taught how to use specific tools to break in somewhere quickly and safely. The 'students' learned to time their crimes precisely, with each participant playing a clearly defined role relevant to the crime in question.

The students were even instructed not to use phones or cars while working: 'Public transport or bicycles are the best way to travel to and from a crime,' revealed one young gangster who had attended the academy when it was still in Romania.

Publicity from numerous high-profile robberies committed by 'students' helped attract even more to attend the academy, which became more popular in the UK than it had been back in Romania.

'They even added more specialist classes on things like being able to spot if you're being followed, as well as understanding forensic evidence,' explained one former 'student'.

And before each proposed robbery, academy members were shown maps and drawings of the target location, plus a secure exit to leave through.

One 'academy trained' gang of foreign criminals in the UK was eventually busted by an organised crime unit from the West Midlands Police, who had access to intelligence on foreign criminal gangs across the globe. But this was a rare breakthrough for detectives.

Meanwhile, the success of Eastern European criminals was hitting the fast-fading old-school British gangs hard. By then they were failing to make even a small dent in the foreign gangs' operations in the UK. Old-school robber Ned explained: 'We was floundering. Here, they were pulling off the sort of capers we turned our noses up at. We'd thought we were invincible on our home territory and then we'd been pulverised.'

While the traditional crimelands of Essex and Kent were being sewn up by mainly Eastern European gangs, the Russian Mafia continued to cash in on their connections to some of the UK's richest and most powerful oligarchs, most of whom were based in London.

As Romanian drug baron Sami explained: 'The Russians keep a distance from all the Eastern Europeans because they work in different circles. But when the Russians want something to happen, it just happens.'

However, the streetwise Eastern European gangs did share one particularly unsavoury criminal activity with the Russians.

5
WOMEN

The constant noise of traffic thundering through the tunnel and across the Queen Elizabeth II Bridge could be clearly heard in a sprawling, almost deserted lorry park close to the looming shadow of The Crossing. In the far corner was a long, rusty red shipping container. It seemed deserted, but had mini-CCTV cameras attached to all four corners of it. Nearby, there were three virtually identical Fiat 500 cars parked up in the far corner of the same lorry park. I knew from my earlier dealings with the foreign gangsters in this area that most of them drove this specific make of vehicle.

As I got out of my car and started walking towards the shipping container, the front driver's door of one of those Fiat 500's swung open and pint-sized Albanian drug lord Bari got out smiling.

'Welcome,' he said, looking up at me and then shaking my hand.

Just then a woman in a business suit got out of the passenger side of the same car that Bari had been in. The woman said something in Albanian to Bari.

'Give her phone,' he said.

I hesitated.

'It's fine,' said Bari. 'We just take no risks with this place. You get phone back when you leave.'

The woman took my phone and then got back in the car and shut the door behind her.

As I followed Bari towards the back of the container, I noticed the rumbling sound of heavy bass coming from inside it. I was nervous, having handed over my phone, but knew it was better not to show it. Outside, the omnipresent, distant thudding of vehicles driving over The Crossing continued, unabated.

Bari swung open the container's double metal doors and turned to beckon me to follow him in. The unmistakable smell of cannabis wafted in my direction.

A few feet inside the container were a pair of plastic see-through double doors like the kind used in hospitals. Through them, I could just make out the distinct blur of three red lights coming down from the ceiling. The floor I was standing on was oily and the rubber soles of my shoes creaked as I stepped forward as Bari held open the plastic double doors.

I found myself walking hesitantly into a small dimly lit area complete with faux velvet walls and lino floor bathed in a red glow, thanks to those overhanging ceiling lights. It was as if I'd just stepped into a twisted secret Aladdin's Cave.

Behind a tiny bar in the corner, two scantily clad women looked up and nodded towards Bari. He smiled back as we approached. I noticed the blueish light of a flickering CCTV monitor near to the women.

'Beautiful girls, yes?' said Bari, beaming proudly. 'We bring container through British customs with no trouble because we tell them it is a film set. But girls come on a different truck, of course.'

The shipping container had been converted into a 'club' for foreign gangsters entering and leaving the UK via The Crossing. This was the place, according to Bari, where gangsters and their friends could 'relax' in the company of women, many of whom had presumably been smuggled in from Eastern Europe. For me it was yet more evidence of the full extent of the foreign invasion of The Crossing.

The faces of the two women at the bar were overly made up and their eyes seemed glazed by drink and drugs. One of them smiled at us like an empty vessel.

Bari then grabbed two bottles of beer from behind the bar and gave me one. 'I promise you, these girls very happy,' he said, as if reading my mind. 'They'd be cleaning toilets if they back in Albania. At least here they make good money and send it to families.'

The two women kept their distance while chatting and giggling away together.

'Clubs like this traditional in my country and all over Balkans. Our men need these places to unwind, to relax, to chill out,' Bari explained.

'But what about the police?' I asked.

'No problem,' he said. 'That's why we use container. We move it around. Every few nights, different place. We re-paint outside of it every month. Police have no idea about this.'

As he took a long gulp of beer, the older woman in the business suit who had taken my phone earlier walked in through the plastic doors.

She introduced herself to me as 'Maria' and spoke perfect English.

'You like?' she asked, nodding at the two women now sitting on high stools at the bar.

Bari laughed.

'Maria is "the mummy",' he explained. 'She looks after all girls.'

'You like?' she repeated, this time pointing directly at the women.

I didn't answer and then Bari interrupted: 'My friend here just visiting. Show him one of rooms, so he can see this is good, clean place.'

Maria grabbed my arm and led me towards a narrow corridor off the main area.

'Don't worry,' she said, 'I just make sure they safe and everyone is happy.'

The corridor had two doors on either side of it. As we walked past one door I could hear the unmistakable groaning sound of sex.

At the next door, Maria knocked hard and then shouted just in case anyone was there.

When no one answered, she swung the door open to reveal a tiny room, just big enough for a single bed, with a small bedside table with a light attached to the wall above it and a cracked basin in the corner.

'You write this place is clean and nice. People here think we lock girls up and treat them like dogs,' she told me. 'This not true.'

The walls of the room were beige and smelt of fresh paint, I think. On the bed were at least a dozen teddy bears and stuffed toys. It was very disarming and felt in many ways as if I'd just stumbled into a child's bedroom. Then I noticed the unused condoms on the bedside table next to a small bin filled with screwed-up tissues. On the edge of the corner basin was an assortment of hair sprays, shampoos, face creams and conditioners.

We left the room moments later.

Back in the bar area, I asked Bari where the women went when they were not 'working'.

'The girls work and live here. They use for accommodation. They no go out for nothing. We feed them, give them cigarettes and free drinks here all night long,' he explained.

To me it sounded as if the women were trapped in this container from hell against their free will. But Bari continued to insist this was not the case.

'Every month we swap girls. These ones either go home or go work in other places. Others come here from their home countries, there are many to choose from.'

He wouldn't explain exactly how the women got into the UK but I presumed they were shipped in and out in trucks.

'Hey, you can call this club pop-up brothel if you like. We pop up all over place!'

Bari continued to insist the women who 'worked' in this container brothel were not sex slaves forced to come to the UK.

'Look, I am not involved in bringing women over here,' he said, slightly irritated. 'That's another man, he do it all. All I know is that women have shit lives back home, so at least here they enjoy themselves and earn good money.

'Sex and crime go together where I come from. These guys drive across Europe, get here and want some relaxation before or after they do their crimes and then go home again.'

He added that the latest location of the brothel container was texted on WhatsApp to all regular customers over a twenty four-hour period before it opened 'for business'. And he assured me this particular container was always within a ten-mile radius of The Crossing.

'It has to be near to The Crossing because many gangsters use this route in and out of UK.'

Taki – another Eastern European criminal I met during the course of my research for this book – told me that the container brothel was often used by sex slave gangs to 'test out' women before moving them on to bigger and more lucrative brothels in London and the rest of Britain.

'If the women can't handle it in those containers then they get sent back to wherever they come from. Is that what you would call sex slavery? Maybe it is.'

UK customs and police have frequently come across examples of sex trafficking involving Eastern European gangsters and they believe that all women who work in these brothels are actually slaves, whose passports have been taken from them so they cannot escape.

Take Madja, a vulnerable eighteen-year-old from Moldova. She was trafficked and then forced into prostitution by a

Moldovan gang who threatened to harm her family if she tried to escape from a brothel in South London, back in 2017.

After Madja was arrested by police following a raid on the brothel, she was sent back to Moldova, but her original traffickers tracked her down to the village where she had grown up. She was then gang-raped, strung up by a rope from a tree and forced to dig her own grave. One of her front teeth was pulled out with a pair of pliers.

Madja was then dragged away by those same gang members and slung into a locked room until her injuries had cleared up. After that, she was re-trafficked first to Israel and later back to the UK. She was eventually rescued from another brothel in the UK many months later and received substantial damages from the Home Office for the way that the UK authorities had forced her to return to Moldova the first time, only to be kidnapped and forced into sex slavery once again.

And these Eastern European criminals are not just selling on women from their home countries to so-called 'regular' brothels in the UK, either. One foreign gang is said to have made hundreds of thousands of pounds over the past five years selling women to Asian criminals based in the north of England. Many of these women are from European Union member countries and have even been forced into sham marriages to Asian men seeking residency in the UK. Other women are sold on to grooming gangs, who then turn them into sex slaves and concubines for wealthy clients.

UK law enforcement investigators believe that at least a third of the females groomed by foreign gangs over the past ten years were under the age of sexual consent. And there's no doubt the Eastern Europeans are the 'market leaders' in this cold-hearted vice 'game'.

Many of the women kidnapped and forced into sex slavery in the UK are originally from Romania. Romanian crime boss Sav explained: 'The Romanian women are considered the most beautiful from the Balkans. A lot of them look Italian or Spanish and are much in demand in the brothels in the UK.'

Ironically, part of the reason the old-school English gangsters were so easily overrun by foreign gangs was because they initially sneered at this type of 'business'.

Former bank robber Ned explained: 'We didn't bother competing with the foreign gangs when it came to vice and stuff like that. We didn't recognise fast enough that brothels are a way to consolidate income and power in the type of underworld that those foreign bastards come from.'

Moldovan criminal Vulo, now based in the Home Counties of England, told me: 'The British gangsters think they are too clever to deal with women. They think it's distasteful. Who cares? This is about money, not feelings.'

I'd first met Vula a couple of years earlier when I was working on a TV documentary exposing the sex slave trade between Moldova and the UK. Vula had admitted working as a pimp – or middleman – in Moldova for a gang operating in London.

'This is big business,' he said. 'Rich Russian gangsters and money launderers in London are also involved because they like Romanian and Moldovan women more than the women from most other Eastern European countries.'

Russian Mafia gangsters – predominantly from President Vladimir Putin's old home town of St Petersburg – helped finance two of the biggest and most upmarket brothels in London's West End because they wanted to choose the type of women for themselves. Vula claimed that the Russian-backed brothels are located in large properties in Central London, originally purchased by gangsters to clean their clients' billions of pounds worth of dirty cash: 'The Russians want to control everything when they are paying for it. It's fair enough, but they get very nasty if you cross them and we just want a peaceful life, you know what I mean?'

A year or so later, those same properties were sold for a vast profit, thanks to London's property boom, and the brothels were opened up at different locations. As a result, law enforcement agencies tend not to hear about them.

'You see? Everything is connected,' said Vula.

And it's not just sex slavery that these foreign gangs specialise in, either. Many older women are regularly smuggled into the UK – often in lorries – to be put to work in illegal factories and as domestic servants. These women are in many cases happy to go along with this because they think they will have a better life in the UK.

Polish gangster Voytec explained: 'This happens a lot with Polish women who're often not considered attractive enough to work in the brothels, so they're sent out to work as cleaners and stuff like that.'

Back in January 2018, thirteen Polish gangsters operating in the UK were arrested by police for running a modern slavery business that involved smuggling twenty women in every week from Poland.

* * *

The Albanians have deliberately struck fear into many communities near The Crossing by making sure that rumours constantly circulate about the 'converted' containers and the killings and beatings connected to them.

Albanian drug lord Bari explained: 'Many Eastern European believe torture is good for enemies. This scares many people, which makes it easy to demand protection money from local businesses and control territories.'

A few days after my visit to The Crossing, Bari showed me a shipping container specifically used by Eastern European gangsters for this purpose. This time the location was a deserted field near a gypsy encampment, about four or five miles from The Crossing itself.

Inside the long shipping container, the floor surface was covered in wooden boards and at first it looked like a mobile gym but on closer inspection there were stocks and a set of whips hanging on the wall: this was a torture chamber.

An extremely tall woman in her mid-forties wearing a tight black mini-dress then appeared alongside us. 'This is my friend Tatiana,' said Bari, in an almost fatherly tone. 'She *very* good at her job.'

Tatiana didn't speak a word of English, so Bari did all the translation. She was a professional S&M mistress with a twist because she was also worked as chief torturer of Bari's underworld enemies. She also carried out 'freelance' commissions for a lot of other foreign gangs.

'Tatiana likes to hurt people so this is fun for her,' Bari explained. 'I brought her from Tirana because she does two jobs here and earns much money.'

He also insisted this particular shipping container torture chamber was often used as a 'normal gym', claiming it was very popular with his Eastern Europeans associates, many of whom like to maintain high levels of fitness after long spells in prison.

'Shipping containers fuckin' brilliant invention,' he added. 'We not exist in this country without them.'

* * *

In London and many of the UK's other main cities, Eastern European gangs have also become experts in setting up 'lower league' brothels not involving the Russians – through Airbnb short-term rentals.

As Bari explained: 'You can't park big truck with shipping container in street in middle of city without getting many parking tickets and causing lot of attention. So, we use Airbnb – it's brilliant for us. The owners never know we turn their apartments and houses into brothels because we run these "businesses" for just few weeks at a time and we use British people to front this up for us. That means most people not know it even existed in first place.'

In many of the UK's biggest cities, it's recognised that Eastern European pimps have now taken over as the 'vice kings'. Indeed, in London's Soho, they have pushed out the Maltese gangsters who were running prostitution rackets in the area for more than sixty years.

Former bank robber Ned explained: 'It's just another example of how good the Eastern Europeans are at making dosh out of all types of crimes. These foreign gangsters are like a tsunami surging through this country, taking anything in their path and making more money out of it than any British gangster could manage.'

Romanian drug lord Sav is proud of his fellow criminals: 'The British are so old fashioned! We are the future of this country, not them.'

* * *

Felicia is the former wife of an Albanian gangster who was killed in a police shootout in Tirana, back in 2000. She now 'manages' one of the busiest Airbnb brothels in London.

'I like it here in England, it's much safer than Albania,' she told me.

Felicia arrived in the UK on a false passport a few days after her husband was killed and has remained here ever since. She explained: 'I had to leave because the police in Albania are very crooked and they wanted to find me and kill me after they shot my husband.'

She claimed that many of her London clients were judges, police officers, lawyers, politicians, even a handful of famous Hollywood actors: 'I'm here to help make the girls safe. I am a woman and they trust me. None of them trust men and I don't blame them,' she explained.

It seems widows of infamous criminals from the Balkans often get preferential treatment from the predominantly male gangster population of Eastern Europe.

Bari explained: 'We respect widows of gangsters more than most women because they have to be strong to survive, so we try to help them.'

In some Eastern European countries, these so-called 'black widows' have ended up even richer than their dead husbands or partners ever were.

Take the onetime supermodel widow of legendary Serbian crimelord Željko 'Arkan' Ražnatović. He was shot down in a hail of bullets back in 2000 but since then his family and his widow have positively flourished. But one must never forget that the majority of women who have arrived in the UK illegally from Eastern Europe are usually penniless and forced to have sex with men to pay off their debts to the smuggling gangs. As British crime vet Ned explained: 'You can't sugarcoat this: they're pimps and they're living off immoral earnings, but the saddest thing of all is that I know a lot [of] old-school villains who now wish they'd got into that game.'

British gangsters have always denied they treat women as badly as their Eastern European counterparts. Some even seemed genuinely shocked at the way the sex slave business has evolved in the UK. But are they really any nicer to women than the so-called new kids on the bloc?

Margi – former wife of an old school Essex gangster – certainly thinks not.

'Women are just decoration in the underworld, whether they're British or foreign gangsters,' she explained. 'We're just there to feed and fuck them in that order.'

However, British gangsters I have spoken to down the years insist they would never work as pimps. Old-time Essex face Billy told me: 'That's the lowest of the low! We look on pimps as vermin. Living off women is not right and we would never do that.'

British old-school gangster Les – who operated near The Crossing until the foreign invasion of his territory – explained: 'The Albanians are the worse. They treat their women like shit! They see them as commodities, even the wives of some Albanian gangsters are forced by their husbands to work in brothels.'

Some of those same wives of Eastern European criminals in the UK are even occasionally kidnapped by rival foreign gangsters when there is a dispute between them.

'The Eastern European criminals here see women as bargaining tools if there's a dispute between them,' added Les. 'They shit on each other as much as they shit on us. We'd never do that, we don't touch people's families.'

A typical example of this ruthless attitude towards women came back in May 2011 when four criminals abducted a missing financial adviser after being told she was a police informant.

A court later heard allegations that Lynda Spence was married to an Albanian, and that she had been secretly recruited by the Scottish Crime and Drug Enforcement Agency (SCDEA) and the UK-based Serious Organised Crime Agency to provide intelligence about him.

Lynda was at that time living with a Ukrainian woman in the Scottish city. This woman turned out to be the former lover of Lynda's alleged husband and just happened to still be in love with him, by all accounts. Law enforcement agencies Interpol and Europol told police in Scotland at the time that they had received intelligence Lynda Spence had fled to Albania with him and was still alive and well. That wasn't correct.

In fact, two Scottish gangsters had snatched Lynda and forced her to don glasses with black tape over the lenses.

The pair then drove their victim to a grotty flat in West Kilbride, Ayrshire. One led her inside while the other one followed with a homemade torture kit of surgical tape, gloves and loppers.

Lynda was bound by her waist and chest to a computer chair with more tape, while one gangster told her chillingly, 'This is an abduction.'

Her final days were spent in terrifying agony, being brutally tortured and butchered in that seedy flat.

Phone records show both gangsters were back in Glasgow by 7pm each evening, but they would then drive back each day to inflict more pain on their prisoner. One gangster would attack Spence while the other one – too tall to fit in the attic – watched from the stairs.

The torture went on for thirteen agonising days with two other gangsters being ordered to 'babysit' Spence between punishment sessions.

On one occasion, Lynda Spence was beaten with a seven-iron golf club until it was twisted. Another time she had her right thumb and little finger cut off. Her toes were also crushed with tree loppers and her hands burned with a steam iron. She was then left sitting helpless in her own blood and faeces while the shorter of the two gangsters visited the attic room for a 'rest', where he would put his feet up and watch TV.

After yet another appalling bout of violence, one of the gangsters dragged Lynda to the bathroom and killed her with a knife. He then cut off her head with a hacksaw and put the bloody remains in the boot of her own silver Vauxhall Astra hire car, which was never found.

The following day, her attackers visited a friend and asked if he had a boat they could use. They claimed to have 'killed a Scouser' who had come looking for them. The gangsters' friend told them the weather was too bad to get out on the water and so they left. It is not known what they eventually did with Lynda Spence's body.

After a lengthy trial in 2013, Lynda's two killers were jailed for a minimum of thirty years for committing what the judge called 'truly monstrous and barbaric' crimes.

Many completely innocent women have been victims of the gang war that raged between the foreign criminals and old-school British villains in the English Home Counties. At the height of the battles a few years back, a woman in Surrey was shot three times by an Eastern European contract killer posing as a pizza delivery man. It later emerged that the victim had been gunned down by mistake. The killer thought his victim was her sister, who was married to an Armenian convicted a year earlier of murdering the self-proclaimed Chechen Prime Minister, Ruslan Outsiev, and his brother, Nazarbek, in their London flat.

* * *

Deep in the Kent countryside, some miles south of The Crossing, lies a rundown hotel which a gang of Bulgarian drug smugglers 'inherited' as part of a drugs debt. The business side of the hotel is run by an English family as a 'front' to prevent any suspicion about the circumstances behind the 'takeover'.

Bulgarian gangster Anton explained: 'We like having a property in Kent. It's easy for us to get to and this place is ideal for some of our "other" businesses.'

Those 'other businesses' include a cannabis farm on three acres of woodland at the rear of the hotel – 'It's perfect for this type of plant,' he explained.

Running the farm for these Bulgarian gangsters is Paulina – the mother of one of them – who was brought over from Bulgaria because of her particular green-fingered skills.

Anton said: 'Paulina is one of the most skilful growers in Bulgaria. Her husband died when she was bringing up a young family, so she taught herself how to grow cannabis to earn enough money to feed them.'

* * *

Today, the tentacles of the Eastern European criminals based in and around areas close to The Crossing reach far and wide, even across international borders.

In early 2018, a gang of Romanian drug smugglers fell out with a team of old-school Kent gangsters based in Southern Spain and all hell broke loose.

Former bank robber Chas explained: 'The Romanians were using the Kent lads in Spain for transporting hash from Morocco to London, but a shipment of it went missing. Well, the Romanians went crazy and accused the Kent boys of nicking it all, even though they denied it. I don't know what the truth of the matter really was, but I did hear that the hash was stolen by another gang of old-school Brits, who were angry with the Romanians for taking over their territory, back in the UK.'

But as Romanian criminal Clef later told me: 'Romanians never forget. That hash belonged to us and if we couldn't get it back then we would make certain people pay in other ways.'

Less than a month after the original shipment of drugs went missing, two men on motorbikes sprayed a hairdressing salon in Marbella, Southern Spain, with bullets. No one was actually killed, but the female owners of the salon turned out to be related to the British gang who had allegedly stolen the hash in the first place.

* * *

The skilful way that Eastern European gangsters in the UK have secured deals to buy cartel cocaine direct from South America has already been highlighted in this book. But the specific role of the cocaine cartels' London 'representative' regarding this unique agreement has never before been revealed.

Carmela is known in the UK's foreign underworld as 'La Patrona' – Spanish for 'lady boss'. She lives in a penthouse apartment overlooking The Thames in Central London within a short distance of Buckingham Palace. Her bosses are the chiefs of a Peruvian drug cartel now reputed to be the biggest cocaine supplier in the Western world.

Today, Carmela is in her fifties but dresses like an over-grown girl gangster in cream velvet tracksuits, with plenty of gold bling and high-heeled boots. Three visits to her plastic surgeon have done nothing to take out the smoking lines on her cheeks and forehead.

There are rumours that she replaced her late husband with a handsome Romanian gypsy criminal, whom she later discovered was bisexual. He then disappeared from all his usual haunts, never to be seen again.

Occasionally, she has to travel down to The Crossing to meet her Eastern European 'partners' to ensure the next shipment of cocaine arrives safely on UK shores. It is usually expertly hidden in items such as cans of food or agricultural machinery but, as Bari said to me, 'There are many other ways to smuggle drugs but it would be stupid to tell you them, wouldn't it?'

Carmela and her three full-time bodyguards dread these trips to The Crossing because they believe she is more vulnerable to an assassination attempt while in the so-called badlands of Kent and Essex. In recent years she has travelled down the Thames by boat to meet her Eastern European 'partners'. The boat itself is usually moored in the East End of London and used as a small nightclub for Latin Americans living in the UK capital. With her three Latino henchmen in tow, Carmela usually arrives at a small quay on the eastern side of The Crossing, less than two miles from the nearby port of Tilbury.

'We all get on well with La Patrona and she deserves much praise for the way she conducts business,' explained Bulgarian drug lord Sav. 'And, most importantly, her cocaine costs us less because it is bought directly from the South Americans.'

Carmela's background gives no clue as to her current powerful position within the Peruvian cartel she represents. In fact, she arrived in London from Colombia twenty years ago and initially worked as a cleaner.

Sav explained: 'Then she fell for a Colombian guy in London who turned out to be a big name in the Cali cartel. They married and had a couple of kids apparently but then he got killed.'

Carmela bravely went to see her husband's bosses and demanded that she be given his job. She'd grown accustomed to a luxurious lifestyle and didn't want to lose it. She quickly proved herself to be even better at being a 'boss' than he was.

'Then the Colombians pulled back from the cocaine business and I thought she'd quit,' explained Sav. 'But no, she got herself the same job with the Peruvians, who were looking for a London representative a few years back.'

The Eastern Europeans say they much prefer dealing with Peruvians to Colombians because they are 'less volatile'. Bari explained: 'The Colombians were more suspicious of us when we dealt with them. We were happy to see [the] back of them when we switched to the Peruvians. It's worked well for all of us.

'There been no trouble between us and if there are work problems, Carmela comes here and calms everyone down. We hope she stays in London for ever.'

* * *

Despite La Patrona's success, women have also found themselves regularly involved in much less-glamorous aspects of the foreign underworld now dominating Kent and Essex. Eastern European gangsters use women – young and old – as so-called 'mules' to smuggle drugs and often other contraband across borders, usually by public transport.

Romanian drug lord Sav explained: 'This is usually only done when there are smaller, specific orders for drugs from wealthy individuals who want them delivered to wherever they are in the world. Some of our clients are extremely rich and they order tens of thousands of pounds worth of cocaine and other drugs at one go sometimes. You need reliable mules to transport those drugs.'

However, many UK-based Eastern European gangs use female mules more to smuggle 'dirty' currency back into the UK from their homelands.

Sav explained: 'We take all our money out of the UK as quickly as possible before the police or our enemies can get their hands on it. Then we divide all the currency into smaller amounts, which have to be brought back to the UK to supplement all our businesses. This is not easy because Eastern Europeans are searched all the time when they come into the UK. So, we often use women from back home who are desperate for money as one-off mules. It makes sense and they are much less likely to be searched by customs.'

Some women couriers – particularly those from Greece and Italy – routinely use false ID in order to travel more freely through Europe.

Maja, twenty-seven, has visited the area in and around The Crossing on at least half a dozen occasions over the past three years. I met her with Bari in a motorway service station in Kent in the spring of 2019, just before she headed back home by road to Albania after bringing £200,000 in cash to the UK. In perfect English she told me: 'I know many Albanians here from being brought up with them back home. They are simply trying to feed their families and make money. They do not take drugs and they behave very respectfully towards women like myself, whom they have known for a long time. I don't mind being a mule for them because I trust them and I will only carry money – not drugs – so I'm less likely to go to prison, even if I am caught by the British police.'

Maja says the £3,000 fee she gets for each shipment of currency she brings into the UK is essential for her to support her family, back in Albania: 'I have a big family and I am the only one earning any money. I need to feed them and I don't think what I am doing is so bad.'

Her overall impression of the UK is skewed to say the least.

'I never stay long when I come into this country,' she said. 'I don't like the attitude of people here. When they hear I'm Albanian, they think I am either prostitute or beggar.'

Some Albanian drug gangs in the UK also use female illegal immigrants as drugs runners and mules if they still owe the criminals money for being smuggled into the country.

'Many of these people were supposed to pay up to €12,000 to be smuggled into the UK, but they often can't afford to pay off that debt so they're forced by the gangs to work for them,' explained Bari.

But, ultimately, it's the bosses who rule every aspect of the UK's foreign underworld.

6
THE GHOST

The man whom many foreign hoods in the UK called 'The Ghost' never used The Crossing in his life, but often flew over it in his Bell helicopter en route from his detached manor house west of London to his chateau in the Loire Valley.

Most foreign gangsters – especially the Eastern Europeans – call their really big, powerful executives 'boss' and it is important to examine them closely in order to understand how they have influenced the UK underworld as it exists today. 'The Ghost' was once one of the richest of them all because he kept away from all the traditional crimes like drugs, robberies and prostitution and stuck rigidly to one illicit activity only: money laundering. One of his former associates provided me with a fascinating insight into the world of this so-called super-criminal, who first hit the big time at the beginning of the last decade when he was laundering his own money and that of many of the billionaire Russian oligarchs, who had flooded into London just after the 9/11 attacks.

The Ghost comes originally from a rundown suburb of St Petersburg, where he went to school with Russian President Vladimir Putin. One of the few criminals who managed to cross the great divide between foreign and home-grown gangsters in modern-day Britain, he liked to keep a low profile despite the yacht, helicopter, Learjet and half a dozen homes across the UK, Europe and the Far East, including a 'tax-exempt' bolthole in Monaco.

By all accounts, The Ghost revelled in his nickname. One of his associates told me: 'He was always laughing about how other villains were so jealous of him. After all, he had more money than sense. He didn't ever need to work again but he was an out-and-out workaholic, so nothing and no one seemed able to stop him.'

The majority of The Ghost's vast income was down to the foreign criminals loathed and detested by so many British hoods. Without them, he would probably have ended up a low-brow member of the St Petersburg Mafia, like most of his contemporaries.

'He had the Midas touch, no doubt about it,' explained another of his closest associates.

At one stage, the mostly UK-based Russian hood was rumoured to be earning in excess of half a billion pounds every year by laundering money for many of the UK's richest and most crooked residents.

'He carefully nurtured connections with the Russian Mafia guys, who were newly arrived in London just after 9/11,' said an associate. 'Many of them worked with or for other Russian and Eastern European gangsters and that enabled The Ghost to be the perfect middleman for them all.'

The Ghost was even reputed to have 'seen off' a number of Russian Mafia money launderers to emerge as the most-trusted 'cleaner' in London a few years into the last decade.

'The fact he was Russian obviously helped him,' continued the associate. 'Other Russian criminals trusted him more because they knew he'd be punished by Putin if he ever stepped out of line. They even got him to hire a few English accountant types because they seemed to think they'd have less trouble with the UK authorities if they used them.'

Indeed, the Ghost turned out to be so astute he eventually persuaded some of the most dangerous Russian Mafia mobsters to use him for money laundering as well: 'That was a very brave move,' explained the onetime associate. 'He even paid the Russian Mafia guys a percentage of every single deal he did to guarantee they'd never go after him or his business.'

Not surprisingly, The Ghost's renowned 'cleaning' services were in great demand from the richest and most powerful oligarchs in London.

His former associate told me: 'He eventually got richer than many of his own clients. You see, he was cleaning for so many billionaires at any one time that he himself ended up with a bigger income than them.

'He had so much money he'd buy brand-new supercars in the morning and sell them on that afternoon with twenty miles on the clock after getting bored of them. But he always made a profit!'

The Ghost was trusted by his extremely wealthy clients in part because he himself kept such a low profile that few people even knew what he looked like, let alone how he earned his millions.

'That's when people started calling him "The Ghost" because his services were renowned but very few people actually knew who he was. He was invisible, even to some of his richest clients.'

The Ghost employed minimal staff, which meant there was less chance of leaks from his organisation. His former associate explained: 'It was all going very well. He had his trusted associates, butlers and chefs on standby round the clock. He was living like a king, but still managing to stay largely anonymous.'

By this time, The Ghost was describing himself as a property developer and philanthropist and in many ways this was true because he bought and sold some of London's most prestigious houses in order to clean big chunks of the dirty money he handled.

His associate continued: 'Then he started mixing with many of London's rich and powerful, including politicians, movie stars and even the Royal Family. Maybe that wasn't such a good idea because a lot of his clients believed he should remain completely anonymous.'

The same associate added: 'By this time, he was investing hundreds of millions in the UK property market every year. This legitimised him in many ways but it also later led to problems when other criminals started to wonder how he'd got so rich.'

The Ghost's vast fortune was built on a bedrock of 'no-need-to-know' money laundering deals with bigtime criminals, tax avoiders and even corrupt presidents of banana republics, as well as a handful of immensely wealthy London-based oligarchs. At one stage, in 2012, there were even rumours he had picked up half a billion dollars in commission for laundering three billion dollars for Vladimir Putin.

'That was when I really started to worry about him,' said the former sidekick. 'He was taking a huge risk dealing with Putin's money because when other criminals heard rumours on the grapevine, they began to sit up and take notice of what he was doing.'

According to sources, Putin then heard that The Ghost had been talking openly about their 'connections'.

'Putin was furious because he didn't want any exposure, especially when it came to him laundering money,' the associate added.

Meanwhile, The Ghost nurtured yet more new clients, this time with close connections inside various governments, including the UK Parliament. The associate went on: 'He believed he was untouchable by this time. The newly arriving "normal" foreign criminals in the UK were not relevant to him, he was only interested in mega-rich clients, who talked in figures of a billion dollars or more. He kept his distance from the Eastern Europeans and they kept their distance from him.'

But then came the stockmarket crash of 2007/8: 'Many of his regular clients lost fortunes and they started to use him less and less.' The Ghost began 'having problems' with the younger foreign criminals, most of whom had invaded the UK much later than him.

His former associate explained: 'His heyday was the first ten years after the oligarchs settled primarily in London and the Home Counties. Then he began pitching for business from the same Eastern European gangsters he had not had any time for before.'

The Ghost believed he could tap into this lucrative new 'marketplace' and make even more money, but he underestimated the type of characters he was going to have to deal with.'

His former associate picks up the story: 'A lot of his new clients were out-and-out Eastern European gangsters and they soon forced him into agreeing to lower percentage commission deals for laundering all their dirty money. It was a much riskier operation than dealing with London's rich and wealthy elite. He wasn't used to this type of bartering and he found it very distasteful at first. The fact he was Russian didn't help much either because the Eastern Europeans didn't trust the Russians because of the troubled history between all their countries.'

But The Ghost desperately needed to maintain his extremely high standard of living, so he accepted the 'rather distasteful' working practices of his new clients.

'He should have known better,' explained his former sidekick.

By this time, the Ghost was laundering the proceeds from many of the UK's most notorious 'street-level' crimes, which meant the authorities were obliged to take a much closer look at him than when he had been working exclusively for some of London's richest residents. And it wasn't just the police who were showing an interest. His associate explained: 'The UK security services were also getting more involved with investigations into criminals at this time. And then there were the tax authorities and his connections to Putin.'

Then, in the middle of all of this, some of the criminals The Ghost was dealing with were offered immunity deals by British law enforcement officers in order to avoid jail.

'It became a nightmare for him,' revealed the associate. 'Here, he was turning billions of dollars and pounds of black money into useable currency and his own clients didn't fully trust him. Word started to get around the underworld that he was a "snitch".

'Everyone began pulling back from him. He went from earning tens of millions a month to virtually nothing almost overnight. Then his name started being mentioned in official circles. People were accusing him out loud of being a money laundering criminal. Even his longstanding oligarch "friends" began backing away from him because they didn't like being publicly associated with criminals.'

And the mainly Eastern European gangsters – who were now The Ghost's main customers – didn't like what they were hearing, either.

His former sidekick explained: 'His business was melting down before his very eyes and he knew that even his new clients from the Eastern European underworld would soon pull away from him if they thought he was a threat to their liberty.'

Soon, some of the most powerful of The Ghost's mainly Eastern European clients announced they were looking for a new money launderer.

Rumours that The Ghost had in fact 'done a deal' with British law enforcement authorities continued to dog him. His sidekick explained: 'Those rumours would not go away. I don't know the truth about it, but none of it was helpful to him.'

It has been alleged that The Ghost's lawyers *did* talk to British law enforcement on his behalf at one stage about some of his own clients in exchange for immunity from prosecution, but the two parties were unable to agree a deal. The Ghost then began trying to sell up all his property in the UK and told friends he intended moving permanently to Monaco. He even got a couple of relatives from St Petersburg into his vast manor house west of London so they could maintain the property until it was sold.

His associate explained: 'He planned to just take off. He had no choice – a lot of people were after him – but departing like that would leave a lot of unfinished business in his wake.'

Not least was the long list of The Ghost's associates who had played a pivotal role in the UK and Europe's money laundering underworld. The final insult came a few days before The Ghost's planned departure from UK soil when debt collectors confiscated his helicopter, which he had intended to use to fly to his bolthole apartment in tax-free Monaco.

He was being frozen out but did he realise too that his life was in great danger?

Then – on 23 March 2014 at his £20 million mansion, in leafy Berkshire – The Ghost paid the ultimate price for his alleged betrayal when his body was found hanging from the doorknob of a bathroom door in what many believe was a classic Russian 'suicide'. As one former Russian Mafia member later explained: 'The idea is to shame the family so that no one will ever speak openly about the victim and his activities after his death. Pretending it is a suicide is the ultimate insult.'

The Ghost's murder was never solved. Those involved are presumed to have left Britain immediately after the killing. Any suggestion of a link to Putin has always been strenuously denied and whoever is responsible will most likely never be brought to justice.

* * *

The Crossing has provided a gateway into the UK for at least 40,000 foreign gangsters in recent years. Many of them are controlled by ruthless bosses who strike fear and trepidation into their own gangs as well as their opponents. But one foreign crime boss above all others knows this territory inside out because he's actually been living in the UK since the 1970s.

Turkish-born Tinag came over with his family from what is now Northern Cyprus after civil war ripped the island apart. It is claimed that the British felt so guilty about their role in the war that they enabled needy families from both the Turkish and Greek sides of this trouble-torn island to move to the UK with no strings attached.

The young Tinag must have seemed particularly in need of sympathy because he was severely disabled after a childhood illness. But that disability did nothing to water down a shrewd, opportunistic and highly intelligent mind.

By the time Tinag reached his mid-twenties, he had already become the leader of a ruthless gang of UK-based Turkish heroin smugglers in partnership with Afghan warlords, who had fought off invasions from the Russians and then the Americans. Tinag's connections in both Turkey and Albania ensured that his shipments of Afghan heroin arrived safely in Western Europe and beyond. By the mid-1980s, he was said to already be worth millions.

Back then, Scotland Yard already had one eye on Tinag, but failed in three successive attempts to prosecute him. By the time many of the foreign gangsters featured in this book turned up on UK soil, Tinag was already a godlike, almost mythical underworld 'boss' who 'ran' North London and most of Essex where he had then moved to, despite still being severely disabled.

Tinag's connection to The Crossing comes through the Albanian Mafia who had tried to set up their own heroin supply route but found it harder than expected. Eventually they joined forces with him. As Albanian drug lord Bari explained: 'Albanians and Turks often worked together. I remember hearing about Tinag first, back in [the] late-1980s. He was not happy when we earlier ran some heroin in the UK without him, so we went to him to agree a deal.'

Somehow Tinag is still thriving today, despite all the other foreign gangsters now working in the UK.

'He's tough character,' Bari added. 'No one challenge his authority so he'll most likely be here for long time yet.'

These days Tinag spends much of his time in a huge detached mansion near the East Anglian coast and Bari says he only visits The Crossing occasionally for meetings with his Albanian partners: 'Tinag hates The Crossing because it helps so many foreign gangsters come here. He also does not like the war between us and the British, either. Tinag also hate the bridge itself. He says it makes him feel sick because he not like heights.'

The bosses from Albania always insist on meeting Tinaq on the Kent side of The Crossing because they like to be able to get back across the Channel to Europe in double-quick time 'in case there are any problems'.

Heroin king Tinag is unique in that he is feared by both the old-school British gangsters and the foreign new boys on the bloc alike.

Former Kent bank robber Terry explained: 'Being disabled makes him even more scary in a way. He has the coldest eyes I've ever seen and although he never gets involved in violence himself, we all know he won't hesitate to have someone topped if they cross him.'

These modern-day foreign bosses – whose soldiers have for years flooded the UK with drugs – come in all shapes and sizes, it seems. We will never learn about most of them because they have proved too clever to ever be caught or exposed while in the UK.

The use of multiple identities certainly helps. As previously mentioned in this book, most foreign criminals operating in the UK never use their real names, which can prove a logistical nightmare for law enforcement. But ultimately, it's these bosses' chilling reputations for violence that do more than anything to prevent them from being exposed. Most of their associates know that if they ever spoke to the police they would undoubtedly end up six feet under.

Occasionally, UK law enforcement authorities do actually manage to haul in a big fish, though.

Albanian criminal Klodjan Copja, thirty – who ran a £60-million cocaine import syndicate – was jailed in the UK in 2017 after his couriers were intercepted meeting drug-laden lorries arriving near The Crossing, in Kent. For three years, British detectives had tracked Copja's movements while meticulously dismantling his Albanian crime empire, which had contributed towards flooding London and the South-East with tens of millions of pounds worth of Class A drugs.

For more than a year after first arresting Copja's couriers and trusted lieutenants and seizing large quantities of cocaine from safe houses, his identity as boss of one of the biggest-ever drugs gangs to target London remained a secret. Like Keyser Söze in the film *The Usual Suspects*, Copja always seemed to be one step ahead of his pursuers. One time – as officers raided a safe house in Earl's Court, West London – they caught sight of a figure being driven past in a car, but were unable to follow him. That was Copja.

Detective Inspector Nick Blackburn, who investigated the Albanian drug lord, later told reporters: 'Copja had no footprint in the UK. He used false documents and multiple IDs and he had no real previous convictions. It was very difficult for us to work out who this individual actually was.'

Copja's luck finally ran out in 2017 on the border between Greece and Albania when he was caught using a false passport. He was extradited, but police only really knew for sure who he was after he had arrived back in the UK and officers took fingerprints.

Police eventually seized 204 kilos of high-grade cocaine belonging to Copja but they remain convinced to this day that he has trafficked as much as 800 kilos, worth an estimated £150 million. He was finally jailed in August 2018 for almost twenty years.

Klodjan Copja prided himself on keeping a low profile despite making fortunes every month from the sale of cocaine. He had rented a modest, anonymous modern flat in Wandsworth, South-West London.

During the UK police's long investigation into Copja they had also uncovered how Albanian criminals in the UK used specially constructed hiding places for cocaine in cars and other vehicles in case they were ever stopped by the police. On one occasion, detectives stopped one of Copja's henchmen and spent many hours examining his vehicle. A detective later said: 'We'd seen the stuff going in, but we just couldn't find it.'

Eventually officers located a mechanism which opened up the dashboard to reveal several kilos of drugs.

UK police never recovered all the cash from Copja's multi-million-pound drug empire. However, they did establish that most of the money went back to Albania and that's where the trail went cold.

The sheer scale of the drug baron's empire summed up the mounting problems faced by senior officers at Scotland Yard and other UK law enforcement agencies when it came to the continued threat from organised Eastern European gangs. UK police even admit that more often than not, it is good old-fashioned luck that leads them to drug hauls connected to Eastern European gangs.

A classic example came in December 2018 when a twenty-three-year-old Albanian ran a red light on Bishopsgate in the heart of the City of London, the capital's financial district.

After the driver presented police with a poor-quality Lithuanian ID, officers searched his car and found thirteen wraps of cocaine in the gearstick casing. The man's sat nav revealed a delivery address in the heart of the City of London.

A few days later, police stopped another twenty-three-year-old Albanian driving in the same area of the City of London. This time, officers found thirty bags of cocaine in the car. The driver – who was later jailed for thirty-two months – had a fake Greek driving licence and told officers he could not remember where he lived. His two mobile phones revealed a list of 18 postcodes and times for meeting.

Albanian drug lord Bari admitted that the City of London is a prime 'sales area' for Albanian cocaine: 'We love rich bankers in the City because they order big amounts of cocaine all the time.'

Another Eastern European drug boss I once interviewed claimed that one of the world's biggest hedge funds based in the City of London regularly bought £50,000 worth of cocaine from him in a single purchase: 'I was worried by this because they were not criminals and if someone at their work ever talked to the police, they'd be in very big trouble. Buying that much cocaine in one order could be construed as bigtime drug dealing by the police if they got caught.'

Most of the Albanian drug dealers operating in the centre of London now work to a special set of 'rules and regulations'. They tend to be employed in so-called 'straight' jobs, often as Uber taxi drivers because that enabled them to travel around the city without causing suspicion.

Bari explained: 'Being Uber driver is perfect cover for dealing drugs. It gives our men freedom to go anywhere in city legitimately, as far as police concerned.'

One UK drugs squad detective told me: 'This is all about work for the Albanians. They just want to earn huge amounts of money and take minimal risks. That's why they try to keep everything as low-key as possible.'

One Albanian drug smuggler, however, broke these so-called golden rules and then paid severely for it. In 2018, Florentino Gonzales was jailed for 24 years after being found in London with thirty kilos of cocaine – worth £3.6 million – hidden in a custom-made cache in the roof of his £200,000 Bentley Flying Spur.

'What an asshole! His bosses so angry with him after he was arrested. Maybe one day they get him inside prison and then, kaput!' said Bari, running a finger across his own neck.

Police and British criminals nearly all reluctantly agree that the Eastern European gangsters currently residing in the UK are here to stay. One retired detective told me: 'These people often come from rundown, war-torn environments. Britain is luxurious compared to what they are used to. They can earn big money here and they don't mind crushing anyone who gets in their way.'

As previously mentioned, much of the cash made from cocaine and other drugs is laundered or immediately smuggled back to Eastern Europe, where it lines the pockets of many of the capos (bosses), who are often men of great wealth and stature in the communities where they live.

* * *

Having lost the turf war with the foreign gangs, the number of British criminals operating in the areas around The Crossing is obviously minimal, but for many years the Hanna brothers managed to be an exception to that rule.

Kent-born and bred Cavan and Jamie Hanna hailed from an area just on the edge of The Crossing, but deliberately kept away from any territories run by Eastern European gangsters. The pair cleverly hid the vast scale of their narcotics empire behind a facade of frugality. It was only when one of their henchmen was spotted in a sports car that their empire began to crumble.

On the surface, the Hanna brothers appeared to be rather unsuccessful property developers, living with their wives and children in townhouses in rural Kent. Jamie Hanna claimed his annual income was £15,000, while his brother Cavan told the Inland Revenue that he earned a more substantial, but still hardly dizzying, £50,000. What the brothers didn't declare was that between them they ran the old school British underworld's biggest drugs empire at that time. They are said to have earned upwards of £120 million a year in a slick operation that the police spent years trying to penetrate.

During that time, the Hanna brothers had used safe houses across south-east England to store and then sell wholesale amounts of cocaine, ecstasy and amphetamines to street-level dealers. They never sold less than £300,000 worth of drugs to any one individual.

'It looked like a clever operation,' old-school Kent drug smuggler Dave told me. 'In and out, in and out ... They hardly ever even got their fingers dirty – that was smart.'

The Hanna brothers never even had to deal with street dealers or others further down the food chain because they only sold their 'produce' to other 'proper' professional criminals. The other key to their success was keeping everything tight knit. They even used an uncle to store their cash for them. Then there was their cousin to courier the money, plus another old British gangster mate to look after their numerous safe houses. But when the all-powerful Eastern Europeans heard about the Hanna brothers' success they eventually came down hard on them. The foreign gangs are alleged to have informed the police about the Hanna cartel because they wanted to 'get them off the streets'.

Bari explained: 'This was during our war with British – we needed to show them that we mean business. Sometimes you have to do these things to stop your enemies. If those Hanna brothers had been smart, they would have pulled out but they didn't, so action was taken.'

Police spent months shadowing the British drug bosses. They took covert photographs and listened on hidden microphones, which recorded conversations between the gang in their cars. And every now and again the Albanians fed detectives more information about the Hannas.

Then officers from the Serious Organised Crime Agency (SOCA) identified the Hannas' cousin Stephen Mee, fifty-one, as a possible drugs associate suspect. They noticed Cavan Hanna, thirty-nine, was regularly meeting Mee, who had a previous conviction for drink-driving. Police decided to stop Cavan's car and search the vehicle. Inside, they found a booklet containing details of what they thought were drug deals, but with this as their only evidence, Hanna could not be arrested. Detectives decided to expand their electronic surveillance on the brothers and their associates. In one taped conversation, Cavan Hanna told Stephen Mee that he was in the clear and intended to continue with a big-money drug deal.

Further surveillance unearthed that the gang's main safe house was at a block of flats in Acton, West London. There, officers spotted Jon Bastable, thirty-seven – a childhood friend of the Hannas – handing a holdall to Raj Koli, a man recruited to launder money for the gang.

Koli, thirty-three, had broken the underworld's 'golden rule' by driving a flashy £200,000 black Ferrari, which had created so much attention that he had ended up being stopped by police. Inside the car was a holdall containing £414,770, sealed in plastic wrapping, which had the fingerprints of Cavan

Hanna on it. Koli was arrested but, in order to allow the operation to continue, the other man – Bastable – was not detained.

Sensing the authorities were closing in on them, the Hannas took preventative action. They moved their safe house and ordered Bastable to stop working for them and not to approach them.

Then disaster struck for the police surveillance team: they completely lost contact with the Hanna brothers, who had cleverly decided to 'go missing'. Just under a year later, they re-emerged when officers discovered they were using a penthouse flat in Alderman House, Greenhithe, Kent, which was overlooked by the Queen Elizabeth II Bridge, part of The Crossing complex.

The flat was in the name of Darren Rankin, who had been using motorcycles to deliver and collect cash from the Hanna operation. It is believed that the foreign gangsters now dominating that area close to The Crossing had once again tipped off the police.

Surveillance officers eventually saw the Hanna brothers together with Rankin, thirty-eight, and Bastable – and decided to arrest them. When officers from SOCA kicked down the door of the safe house, they found the Hanna brothers and Bastable 'knee-deep' in £1.1 million worth of bank notes.

Two days later, the officers visited another of the Hannas' safe houses in Waterstone Park, Kent, also close to The Crossing. In the garage was a manhole cover. Officers lifted the cover to find two safes, which had been placed there in concrete. Inside, they found £2.7 million in cash, again sealed in plastic. But, like the cash found in Koli's car, it contained fingerprints that turned out to be those of Jamie Hanna.

Another subsequent raid at a warehouse in Abbey Wood, South-East London, uncovered more drugs and cash. Then officers raided yet another house and uncovered 15,000 ecstasy tablets and 80kg of amphetamines. The drugs were valued at £1 million.

Later, CCTV footage taken from a camera overlooking that same target building introduced the SOCA team of surveillance detectives to Martin Winter, forty-six, another member of the Hanna gang. He had been hired by their friend Mee and was the only member of the gang to use drugs recreationally.

Finally, officers visited the home of the Hanna brothers' uncle, George Webb, sixty-one, in Eltham, South-East London, after Jamie Hanna had been spotted by a surveillance team visiting the property.

A search by police eventually unearthed £650,000 in cash in the water tank of the house's loft. In total, £5,131,211 was recovered, but officers believed this was a drop in the ocean compared to what the Hanna brothers had earned over previous years.

One SOCA officer – who could not be named for operational security reasons – later admitted: 'We have never seen a Mr Big of this magnitude and the fact that they have pleaded guilty says a lot: organised criminals of this level do not plead guilty unless the evidence is very daunting.'

The Hanna brothers, along with six others, were eventually given heavy prison sentences. In their case, fourteen years each. Some British gangsters believe they may seek revenge on the Eastern Europeans, if and when they are released from prison.

Despite their arrest and subsequent sentencing, the British Hanna brothers were indeed a rarity in the Kent and Essex underworld by this time. Further afield, the foreign gangsters were also making big moves within the rest of the UK underworld.

Albanian drugs kingpin Khalad Uddin was the national coordinator, facilitator and link to an elaborate narcotic network spanning right across the Black Country, Oxford, London and Bristol. Police specially launched Operation Stingray to try and catch him.

The thirty-five-year-old was yet another who made the classic mistake of living a lavish lifestyle, with a plush apartment in Oxford that cost £28,000 a year to rent. He also drove a fleet of seven luxury cars, including a Range Rover and a BMW 7 Series. Once again, by flaunting his wealth he flagged himself up to the police, otherwise he would probably never have been noticed.

Investigators then discovered £442,000 in cash during a raid at Uddin's office property and his family home, both in Oxford. A ten-tonne hydraulic press – believed to be used to package cocaine – was also found in one of the bedrooms of Uddin's home.

It eventually emerged that he was the ultimate middleman, receiving 1kg packages of cocaine from a London-based Albanian drugs gang and then selling those drugs 'wholesale' to dealers in the Midlands on behalf of two Albanian bosses.

In October 2018, Uddin eventually admitted two counts of conspiracy to supply drugs and one count of money laundering. He was already serving a fourteen-year prison term, having been found guilty of firearms offences earlier. But police believed that he had stashed tens of millions of pounds away from his drugs business and that the majority most likely ended up back in Albania.

One of Uddin's associates – another Albanian criminal, Erald Mema, thirty-three – was later jailed for twenty-five years after being found guilty of conspiracy to supply cocaine following his trial at Oxford Crown Court. The court learned that the cocaine Uddin and Mema sold had a purity range of between 60 and 91 per cent.

Mema was the 'linkman' who travelled between Albania and the UK. The police alleged that Mema, of Nursery Close, Botley, and Uddin – from Little Brewery Street, Oxford – together ran a massive drugs distribution network.

Today, UK police have dubbed Albania 'the Colombia of Europe' as it has now been recognised as being the entire continent's drug trafficking headquarters. No wonder the Adriatic Sea – which separates Albania from Italy – has become virtually a highway for drug trafficking. Elsewhere, Albanian gangs have recently started purchasing Chinese manufactured synthetic cannabis – recognised by many as being more harmful to health than real hash.

'The Albanians just go from strength to strength,' said one recently retired British drugs squad officer. 'It's not just cocaine or cannabis, either. They don't care what they handle – even heroin – as long as there is a healthy profit to be made.'

Nothing, it seems, is too big a deal for the Eastern Europeans as they continue to manipulate police, local politicians and even public service officials in their own country.

'In many ways Albania is the nearest thing to a narco state in Europe and I can't see that changing any time soon,' said one European drugs expert.

Even on the streets of Albania's capital Tirana, the impact of the drug gangs is clear to see, thanks to the numerous expensive detached houses in the city suburbs. Three gang bosses there are said to own a chain of old people's homes which house elderly criminals, who are often used to smuggle cash in and out of Britain in exchange for their board and lodging. Yet on paper, Albania remains one of the poorest countries in the Western world with the nation's banks owing billions in debt. Many Albanians say these gangsters bring tens of millions back into the economy and, as a result, they're often welcomed home with open arms.

'They spend big money on houses, cars, women. This all helps our country's finances,' said Albanian drug lord Bari. He is certain, though, that he would prefer to be arrested and imprisoned in the UK.

'Being in prison is part of job,' he explained. 'At least here in UK, sentences not long and you always get out early for good behaviour. Back in my country, conditions are shit and sentences always fully served. It's better to get arrested here.'

While the war between the Eastern Europeans and the old school UK gangsters may be over, fresh skirmishes between these bitter enemies continue.

'Sometimes we have to make an example to show British they must not challenge us. Often that means taking out someone big, like one of their bosses,' Bari explained.

7
ARMS RACE

Peering through a small hole in a garden fence in Essex while watching his target's every move was a young Eastern European criminal, who just a few hours earlier had picked up a Skorpion machine pistol from a notorious arms dealer based near The Crossing. The man spent many days through the early summer of 2015 studying the layout of the garden and the surrounding parkland. His target was an infamous veteran sixty-three-year-old British career criminal, who had finally pushed his luck too far. The young criminal had even been supplied with a sketch of the target's garden featuring the location of each CCTV camera and the areas where the cameras did not reach.

He continued watching as the elderly British criminal finished a call on his mobile phone and then got back on his quad bike and drove thirty yards to collect leaves and wood to put on a nearby bonfire. A few seconds later, the man put the rubbish on the bonfire before driving off again on his quad bike to the other end of the garden.

There, he got off the quad bike, walked across to a small garden shed and entered it. Moments later, the British criminal emerged with large bundles of paperwork in his arms. He dumped it all onto the back of the trailer, drove back to the bonfire and began feeding the flames with the documents.

The man in the garden was about to make a call on his GPS 'spy-proof' mobile phone when he glanced back at his house, just as one of his two dogs leapt up at the window, barking noisily in the direction of his master. He smiled, but said nothing.

Back behind that fence just a few yards away, the watcher's eyes snapped around in all directions. He was picking up sounds and sights that most people wouldn't even notice. Even lumps of horse manure near the fence had earlier been expertly avoided.

The young criminal already knew the far corner of this garden near the dustbins wasn't covered by the CCTV cameras. He crouched down and looked through the hole in the fence once again as he waited for the perfect moment. Light drops of rain began pitter-pattering on the green foliage in the dense shrubbery and woodland surrounding him.

Back in the garden, his intended target had just fed his fourth trailer-load of leaves and paperwork onto the fire when his mobile rang once again. On the other side of the fence, the watcher heard his target's voice as he answered it.

Observing through that hole in the fence, the man removed a self-loading lightweight Skorpion machine pistol containing smooth-bore .32 calibre bullets from the large outside pocket of his jacket. He then glanced at his watch before expertly attaching a silencer onto the end of the barrel.

The elderly British criminal walked to the spot away from his bonfire not covered by the CCTV cameras, so he could speak without fear of surveillance. It wasn't a long call this time. He had just switched off his phone when the watcher leapt silently over the fence and pointed his gun directly at his target.

For a few moments, both men stood and stared at each other.

The muffled sound of the dogs barking could be heard in the distance.

Then the younger man squeezed the trigger.

Three bullets pierced the older man's body instantly, sending him crashing to the ground. Only a dull thud could be heard with each shot, thanks to the silencer.

The bullets contained wires specifically designed to fragment and inflict maximum damage on internal organs, as well as ensuring that external bullet wounds would not be clearly visible.

Inside the house, the two Dobermanns barked ever louder.

In the garden, the target lay crumpled on the ground, trying to breathe. He began crawling slowly across the grass towards the decking near the dustbins. The shooter watched him for a few moments. Then he glanced casually down at the elderly man's back, squeezed lightly on the trigger and three more bullets hit the target.

The shooter's eyes then panned 360 degrees to check for witnesses as the sweet, musty smell of cordite must have wafted through the air. He suspected there were other people inside the property but no one had stirred.

Before the shooter departed, he checked the ground for any evidence he might have left behind. Then he casually jumped over the fence, strolled through the undergrowth and back onto the pathway used by horse riders before picking up a stolen bicycle he'd left leaning against a tree and headed onto the main road.

The use of that bicycle was seen as significant evidence that the shooter most likely had been 'trained' at the same crime academy now run near The Crossing after being first opened in Bucharest, Romania.

'The low-key nature of the way that guy left the scene means he must have been Eastern European and most likely attended the academy at some stage,' said one Essex police source.

Less than half an hour later the same killer drove over the Queen Elizabeth II Bridge on The Crossing and made his way down towards the Channel ports of Dover and Folkestone and onto the badlands of Europe and beyond.

His victim had been a onetime stolen gold bullion fence-turned-timeshare multi-millionaire who had upset two of the most powerful new foreign faces working inside the UK by allegedly double-crossing them on a drugs deal. Police investigating the murder soon realised one of the keys to solving this cold-blooded slaying would be to trace the gun used in the attack. But that would not be easy: the recent influx of foreign criminals into the UK meant that weapons like these were readily available throughout the crimelands of Kent, Essex and London.

Especially in the vicinity of The Crossing.

* * *

Although he refuses to confirm or deny it, there is a more than a reasonable chance that the Skorpion machine pistol Essex police believe was used to kill the elderly British criminal came from one particular 'specialist' underworld armourer, who works near The Crossing.

We'll call her 'Ray' but she used to be known as 'that fuckin' woman cop' to British gangsters in reference to her former profession. These days Ray's most important clients mainly come from Eastern Europe. She also claims to have been the first underworld arms dealer in the country to supply the Skorpion to her underworld 'clients'.

Ray got her first supply of Skorpions from demobbed British soldiers who fought in Kosovo during the 1990s Balkans conflicts. Some of these weapons had allegedly been stolen by the squaddies from the corpses of their enemies.

Today, the Skorpion is so well known in the ganglands of Eastern Europe that it has become the must-have weapon for mobsters.

Gun dealer Ray runs her business from a rusty green container, which sits at the end of the garden of a house she owns on the outskirts of Dartford, Kent.

'She only works in daylight so everyone knows her opening hours,' explained Keith, an old-school British gangster who has known Ray for more than thirty years.

Ray's underworld armoury has been talked about in southeast England since long before foreign gangs began to operate in these parts. She even kept a two-acre field deep in the countryside south of The Crossing, where she ran an illicit shooting range so that her clients could test out weapons, if they so wished.

Some inside the old school local underworld believe that Ray's past will one day come back to haunt her, but for the moment, she brushes it off.

'Ray's a tough nut, especially for a woman,' explained her friend Keith. 'But she's seen it all. One gang of Albanians tried to force her to hand over her armoury a few years back because they believed she was a police informant.

'Ray laughs about it now but it was a pretty heavy situation at the time. At one stage, the Albanians kidnapped her from her armoury and threatened to kill her if she didn't hand over the business but she refused to budge and in the end they respected her for it. So, they let her carry on running her armoury and Ray's now even on really good terms with them, which is a testament to what a great operator she is.'

Some British old-school criminals remain convinced that the Eastern Europeans are 'running' Ray's business and she is nothing but a convenient local 'frontperson'.

'That's bollocks!' responded Keith. 'Ray knows how to play them all off against each other. They're the ones who should watch their backs.'

He believes that many local gangsters have disliked Ray since many years ago when she recruited a gang of Romanian criminals to protect her when she fell out with a well-known North London crime family.

'That was a shrewd move by Ray,' he explained. 'The gang she'd fallen out with hated foreigners and were terrified of the Romanians. In the end they all agreed a peace treaty and there's been no trouble between them since.'

But it is Ray's previous career in the police which obviously makes her such a unique character to be based so close to The Crossing. Ray was dismissed from the police in the mid-1980s after being caught red-handed supplying a confiscated gun to a well-known British robber in a South London pub. She claimed to police bosses that she was trying to recruit the man into becoming an informant, but that didn't wash with her superiors and she was 'eased out' of the job.

Keith recalled: 'Ray left the police at a time when every other bobby was on the make but no one expected a lowly woman police constable to be crooked. She even managed to hold onto her police pension because the bosses at Scotland Yard didn't want to admit how bent all her other colleagues were as well.

'The top brass at the Yard tried to brush it all under the carpet because they were embarrassed by just how institutionally corrupt so many officers were, back in those days.'

Today, Ray has even adopted the criminal habits of her mainly Eastern European customers by using a shipping container as her 'shop'. Keith explained: 'For years Ray operated out of various properties but then this Albanian fella came to see her and said he wanted Ray to supply him with three guns each and every month but a condition was that she ran her business from a container, so that it could be moved around regularly.'

When Keith last saw Ray, that container sat in the garden of one of fifteen properties owned by her within a twenty-mile radius of The Crossing. 'She even does short-term gun rentals to a lot of the younger Eastern European lads – they all pay cash and then return the weapons on their way out of the UK.

'Ray says that being a gun supplier and a woman is very challenging but I think she thrives on it in a way,' said Keith. 'And she says her income has gone up ten times since the foreign gangsters appeared round here. It just doesn't bother Ray to be dealing with the foreigners. She's in the business of supplying arms, she don't care who her customers are as long as they pay her on time.'

Keith says the inside of Ray's container is like a darkened weapons cave. Some guns hang on the walls, others are kept in fridges, and small arms even hang on the inside of cupboard doors. 'She's got a weapon for all occasions,' he said with a chilling smile.

Once night-time falls, Ray shuts up shop and heads for her isolated, detached mansion in the heartlands of Kent, halfway between The Crossing and the channel ports of Dover and Folkestone. No one knows if Ray has a family because she keeps her private life under wraps.

'She always keeps in touch with her main customers by WhatsApp so that they know where the container will be on any given day. It's a good failsafe system, which cuts right down on the chances of a raid by the police.'

Keith insists that Ray still has 'friends' in both the Kent Constabulary and London's Metropolitan Police, but none of them know about her role as an underworld armourer: 'They know she did a few dodgy deals after she quit the cozzers, but they don't know about all this stuff.'

He also insisted she didn't feel responsible for any of the victims who might end up being shot with the weapons she supplied: 'I asked Ray that once and she said, "Listen, I don't pull the trigger and most of the time my guns are used as a threat, not a reality. That's how it works with criminals. They need guns to get what they want but the last thing they want to do is actually shoot someone."'

Keith says that the Scorpion machine pistol is without doubt the most popular gun Ray has ever sold and he himself waxes lyrical when talking about it.

'That little beauty was first built back in 1959 by the Czechs,' he explained. 'They really knew their stuff back then. They banged out tens of thousands of them from a factory near Prague.'

The Skorpion is an ultra-light machine gun which can be fired with one hand, a big plus factor. It's ideal for security forces and special forces but the Czech army adopted it and this helped spread the Scorpion's reputation around the globe, helping it become the weapon of choice for many gangsters.

Overall, it is capable of 850 rounds per minute, which would be devastating in a terror attack or even a bank robbery. In recent times it has even been used by contract killers because it fires so many bullets so quickly that it 'guarantees' instant death.

The Scorpion usually comes with a folding shoulder stock made from steel wire as well as a leather pistol-type holster and magazine pouches.

Keith explained: 'These days, armed forces personnel in many countries use the Scorpion as a sidearm but over the years it's also been manufactured in other countries such as Yugoslavia, which is why so many of them are now floating around.

'I particularly like the newer models with synthetic grips instead of the wooden ones from the 1960s. There is even a civilian version known as the M84A and this has sort of legitimised the use of the Skorpion as an everyday weapon of choice.'

In recent years there have been efforts to more closely track Skorpions by the authorities but with so many now in circulation, it is virtually impossible. Production ended in the early 1990s as the walls of Communism came down but by that time there were so many different versions of the weapon in circulation that keeping track of individual guns became a logistical nightmare.

'Ray may be getting on a bit now,' said Keith proudly. 'She's in her late sixties but she's still top in her field, which is why the Eastern Europeans nearly always go to her.'

These days Ray is seen more as a divisive figure by many old-school British criminals because of her open connections to the Eastern Europeans.

'They just don't understand her,' said Keith. 'Obviously it's partly cos she's a lady and they underestimated her in the first place. Now they can't handle the way she has more balls than all of them put together.

'When Ray first started out in this game, a lot of English villains thought she was planted in this job by the cozzers. Then they gradually got over that. Now they don't like her cos she sells to the foreign gangsters.

'Ray told me that in many ways the Eastern Europeans are much better to deal with than the old Brits. They treat her with much more respect. The foreigner gangsters don't drink or take drugs and they're incredibly focused. They always pay on time and they know exactly what they want. The old-school British villains, on the other hand, are much more tight-fisted and tricky to deal with. A lot of them also moan and groan about their miserable lives and how much better it was before the foreigners turned up.

'Ray's had many more run-ins with old-time Brits in recent years than the foreigners because they're just not on the modern wavelength when it comes to crime. No wonder the foreign guys are cleaning up here!'

The Crossing is an integral part of Ray's gun business because it is at the epicentre of so much criminal activity.

Keith explained: 'A lot of villains come back and forth over The Crossing. Ray always keeps her container within a six- or seven-mile radius of it because she picks up a lot of business that way.'

He also claimed that she was much 'safer' today because of the foreign criminals who are her main customers: 'In the old days, the British gangsters were easy for the police to infiltrate, which meant much bigger risks for Ray. Today, the police have given up trying to bust most of the foreign gangs because they can't infiltrate them at all as they come from other countries. That means much less risk for Ray. She's become virtually untouchable.'

But many of the old-school British gangsters from these parts remain bitter about gun dealer Ray. Former bank robber Teddy told me: 'Just cos she's a fuckin' woman, she thinks she can get away with it. But she's not loyal to her people and that's out of order. She should only work for us. After all, we protected her for years after she was thrown out of the police. Now she's arming the foreigners, who are then pointing their guns at us.'

I recently picked up on a rumour about Ray that if true might come back to haunt all the criminals – both foreign and English – whom she has dealt with. One former Kent police-man told me: 'A lot of us remember Ray from when she was still a copper and, actually, she was a damn good officer in many ways and we were all very surprised when she turned out to be dodgy. But not long ago I was talking to someone in a pub who also used to work with Ray and he told me that Ray had something very surprising up her sleeve: she's actually been working undercover for police in London and Kent for years.

'If that's true then it looks as if Ray has had the last laugh on all of us. It might also help to explain why she has managed to avoid arrest for so long. But I'd like to know how she can be working for the police and still selling weapons that end up being used in major crimes. I appreciate that if this is true, she can't break cover. But surely there is a limit to how she can still operate as a criminal and get away with it, if she's supposed to be working for the cozzers?'

As they say in the trade, only time will tell.

* * *

Other criminals on both sides of this ongoing underworld war on UK soil say that loyalty is irrelevant when it comes to this new, chilling gangster empire. Some Eastern European gangsters even ignore weapon suppliers like Ray and smuggle their own arms into this country by boat. And when they do this, they will sometimes even use washed-up British gangsters to handle the arms shipments because they're less likely to create suspicion.

'If you are an Eastern European man coming into UK by car, plane, boat, whatever, you always get searched,' said Albanian drug lord Bari. 'It's better to use English men to bring in guns, they less likely to be stopped.'

Weapons are also often smuggled into the UK through florists' lorries from Holland, which arrive in the Kent ports every day with fresh flowers for thousands of shops across the country.

Overall, the number of arms circulating in Britain these days has reached epidemic proportions. Some foreign gangs even sell weapons in the UK themselves because they can access arms so easily in their home countries and consider the UK to be a lucrative marketplace. And when British gangsters try to compete with foreign gangsters in the UK it usually ends in tears. When two young Kent gangsters sailed their motor cruiser *Albernina* up the Medway river near The Crossing and then towards a marina on the outskirts of Rochester, little did they know they were already under law enforcement surveillance after an illegal arms deal in France less than twenty-four hours earlier.

On board that vessel in August 2018 were twenty-two Czech vz.58 assault rifles, similar to the AK-47, and nine Skorpion machine pistols, along with fifty-eight magazines and more than 1,000 rounds of ammunition. The guns had been previously deactivated in Slovakia, but were then reactivated before being acquired by the two British criminals. They had then been loaded onto the *Albernina* in Boulogne-sur-Mer, France, before sailing to Kent.

Moments after docking in Kent one of the young British gangsters quoted The Notorious B.I.G. lyrics when he emailed: 'We now officially gangsters' and his associate on board replied, 'Fucking nice one!'

'Hahahaha defo that's sick. Duck and run for cover bitches. We are a firm aint we', and his friend responded: 'Proper heavy and armed to the teeth no one wants beef fam.'

Then one of the men exchanged messages with a mystery contact, 'B', to arrange the onward supply of the guns and bragged he was a 'proper cartel'.

The two gun smugglers were using mobile phones with encrypted software PGP – Pretty Good Privacy – and referred to guns as 'toys' and bullets as 'sweets' in an attempt to evade incriminating themselves. Both men from the boat, plus another British criminal who was waiting at the dock, then went straight to a nearby Homebase store to buy bags and tools before burying the guns until they were needed, with the intention of later offloading them to other gangsters.

But a team of detectives from the National Crime Agency had been watching their every move. Minutes later, the officers swooped and arrested the three men and seized their deadly cachet of arms before the gangsters even had time to bury their weapons.

Later in court it emerged that one of the British men had masterminded the plan and paid for the guns, helped by a foreign gangster in Europe. Although the gang had no connection with terrorism, the source and route of the weapons had been the same as those used in the earlier Charlie Hebdo atrocity in Paris, the NCA later told a court.

Both men on the boat were eventually found guilty of gun smuggling and possessing firearms with intent to endanger life after an Old Bailey trial held amid almost unprecedented security. Ring leader Shilling was sentenced to thirty years plus five years on an extended licence. The other main gang members got nineteen years each.

Two of their associates admitted helping the men and were imprisoned for conspiracy.

Afterwards, Rob Lewin, National Crime Agency (NCA) Head of Specialist Operations, told reporters: 'The weapons seized here were hugely powerful and the evidence showed that the gang would have had no hesitation in using them. They thought having this kind of firepower made them untouchable, but we were determined to stay one step ahead of them all the way.'

Other British gangsters have fared just as badly after trying their hand at gun smuggling in recent times. In 2017, a low-level three-man British gang tried to smuggle stolen arms, including a pistol and two sub-machine guns, into the country using a hired van. Armed officers from the Sussex Police Serious Crime Unit stopped the vehicle on the off-slip road at junction 10 of the M23 southbound in Crawley, near Gatwick Airport.

Police found a self-loading Walther P38 pistol, two reactivated Czechoslovakian Skorpion sub-machine-guns and ammunition all wrapped in plastic tape and attached to the van with magnets.

Three British criminals eventually pleaded guilty to importing and possessing with intent to endanger life. The men all received sentences of between twelve and sixteen years and two months. But even more disturbing for the small old-school criminal contingent who are still trying to operate in and around The Crossing, there is credible evidence that Eastern European gangsters tipped off the police about both of the British gun smuggling operations reported here.

Old-school criminal Tom told me: 'I heard the foreigners were pissed off that the British boys were trying to muscle in on the arms game, so they got them nicked. How evil is that? Where I come from, that is crossing the line.'

From the streets of Eastern Europe to the pockets of gang members in British cities, the illegal trade in firearms continues to supply the UK's increasingly violent criminals with the weapons they need to wreak havoc. In the last five years, the annual number of recorded crimes involving firearms has risen from just over 5,000 to more than 6,600. The NCA believe the typical route taken by a firearm starts with production in the former Soviet bloc, through ports either side of the English Channel to the housing estates of British cities, where the same weapons often claim the lives of warring gangs and innocent people caught up in the carnage. It seems no amount of tough new UK regulations can stem this demand amongst criminals for guns.

'The trouble is that "being tooled up" [armed], as we used to call it when I was a villain, has become normal practice today,' explained onetime Essex robber Charlie. 'Back in the 1980s, we only ever carried a weapon if it was absolutely necessary. Now all the young gangsters see what's happening with the foreign teams and believe they have to be armed all the time for their own protection. It's like the Wild West out there.'

Within the UK it is claimed that some weapons can fetch thousands of pounds if the weapon is rare: 'If it comes with magazines and ammunition, that also massively increases its value,' onetime robber Vince told me. 'Obviously, we're talking top-of-the-range models here for the big boys. There's plenty of rubbish guns around too.'

Gun dealer Ray's big seller – the Skorpion machine pistol – can be bought for not much more than a few hundred pounds on the Eastern European arms market and then sold for thousands in the UK.

In 2018, Eastern European arms traffickers were reported to be offering gangsters in the UK two-for-one deals on guns, automatic weapons and grenades.

'The foreign lads don't even care about supplying arms to the Brits, even though they're now big enemies when it comes to so many territories in Kent, Essex and London,' said Vince. 'They'll soon be another war out there and guns will have fuelled it. I wouldn't want to be a criminal in today's Britain. You won't live long, that's for sure!'

As far afield as Scotland, police have uncovered weapons used in shootings linked to foreign gangland feuds. These guns have originated from countries including Romania, Bulgaria, Slovakia, Serbia, Albania and Montenegro.

One of the UK police's rare successes in trying to stem the tide of weapons coming into the country came in October 2018 when a gang of Eastern Europeans was jailed for eighty-five years after smuggling dozens of firearms, including handguns, six sub-machine guns and more than 5,000 rounds of ammunition, into the UK from Germany between January 2016 and March 2017. The ultra-violent gang even managed to get some of their illegal firearms onto the streets of the UK's biggest cities, including London, before they were arrested. Other weapons were eventually seized from addresses across the country following a massive fifteen-month-long investigation.

UK police first uncovered the arms smuggling ring two years earlier when officers stopped a Nissan Patrol SUV in London and found some weapons hidden by the front axle. Detectives then raided properties in Sheffield, in South Yorkshire, St Albans and Watford, Hertfordshire, where many more weapons were uncovered from secret stashes.

All the men involved pleaded guilty at their trials in 2018 and received long prison sentences after they were convicted of conspiracy to sell or transfer firearms and ammunition. The lengthy sentences imposed by the judge showed just how seriously the courts were dealing with these offences.

Another case busted wide open by police involved a gang of Pakistani men from Luton, north of London, who had plotted to bring guns into the UK. In March 2016, a number of guns and ammunition were recovered by police after they were supplied to a criminal group based in Leicester, in the Midlands, by the Luton gang.

A joint surveillance operation between the Special Operations Units in East Midlands and the Eastern Region (EMSOU and ERSOU) uncovered the supply of three Hungarian FEG semi-automatic handguns and twenty-one rounds of ammunition.

ERSOU officers discovered that the head of the group had sourced these weapons in the Netherlands before using other gang members to provide security, package and store firearms, collect money and deliver the weapons to other criminal groups.

Dutch police and the NCA officers helped stop two of the group at the French border and guns were found hidden in a hired Ford Mondeo.

The group itself had used more than sixty mobile phone numbers over a four-month period to try and cover up their criminal activities. They were eventually sentenced to more than eighty years' imprisonment.

In London, many senior police officers are reluctant to name foreign gangs as causing the current spike in gun violence for 'political correctness' reasons.

'It's fuckin' ludicrous!' said one retired London detective. 'The world's gone PC mad! The police are afraid to upset a suspect before he's even been arrested. But the facts are that a lot of these foreign gangs are using way more guns than existed before they came.'

Scotland Yard's Trident unit – which investigates gangs in the capital – recovered more than 700 live firing weapons in 2018, the majority of which had a link in some way to foreign gangs. A senior officer said: 'The weapon is often used as a mechanism to protect your Class A trade — and Class A is the lifeblood of gangs and organised criminal networks.'

Border officials and police are clearly struggling to hold back the tide of weapons entering the country.

'The number of cases involving gun smuggling just shows how prevalent this problem is in the UK today,' one recently retired Scotland Yard detective told the *Daily Mail*. 'And you can be sure that for every case brought to court, there are many other weapon-smuggling gangs bringing guns into this country with impunity.'

* * *

On the south coast of the UK, between Kent and East Sussex, there are numerous fishing and recreational vessels which make ideal boats for smuggling arms and other contraband.

In the seaside town of Hastings – just a few miles west of the border between the two counties – a fisherman called Lenny told me that he was constantly being approached in local pubs by both British and foreign gangsters wanting him to smuggle drugs or stolen arms on his vessel.

'It happens all the time,' he explained. 'And I have no doubt there are fisherman here in this community who do smuggle drugs and guns in order to survive. There isn't much money to be made out of honest fishing these days.'

Lenny and many of his fishermen colleagues have also heard stories about stashes of drugs being found floating in the sea or caught up in fishing nets.

'It's never happened to me personally but I would be sorely tempted to take the drugs and try and sell them if I found them myself,' he admitted.

The family of one fisherman further up the coast near Eastbourne were kidnapped by a foreign gang, who then forced the fishermen to pilot his vehicle out to sea for a drugs pick-up.

'That was really heavy,' Lenny recalled. 'They went round to see his wife and kids and sat them down and made sure they couldn't leave until the boat came back with drugs.'

In 2017, two fishermen working on the south coast of Kent discovered a stash of cocaine worth £20 million floating in a buoy.

Lenny explained: 'Apparently, they handed it in because they were scared the criminals who owned it might come after them if they tried to sell the drugs themselves. In the drug business you get severely punished if you try to sell other people's produce.'

Also in 2017, foreign gangsters packed 255 kilograms of cocaine into eleven watertight holdalls and left them floating in the sea after being dropped from a container ship travelling from Brazil to Antwerp. Other members of the same UK-based gang then set off from the Isle of Wight in a boat owned by a lobster fisherman to collect those packages.

Following a tip-off from the UK coastguard, the fishing boat was being tracked by a UK Border Agency vessel. The crew then found the holdalls attached alongside a rope in a similar style to lobster pots, with a buoy and a makeshift anchor tied to either end. The gang were then watched by police gathering up the parcels from the lobster pots.

Officers from the Serious Organised Crime Agency and the Metropolitan Police then swooped. Four men were arrested, including an Albanian national whom police believe had financed and organised the entire operation. The gang ended up being jailed for a total of 104 years for conspiracy to import the Class A drug.

Chris Farrimond of the Serious Organised Crime Agency told reporters: 'These men ran it like a commercial fishing expedition. Rather than bringing them massive profits, however, their plan has put them in the same unenviable position as many others who have been caught attempting to traffic drugs under the guise of legitimate business.'

Meanwhile, the so-called peace treaty between the Eastern Europeans and the old-school British gangsters remains on a knife edge.

'It just takes one incident and all sorts of trouble flares up again,' explained retired bank robber Ned.

A classic cause of such 'problems' can occur when drugs either go missing or are seized by the authorities, as was the case after 4.2 tonnes of cocaine was uncovered off the coast of South America, back in 2016. The drugs – worth more than £150 million – were on a 70-foot flagged fishing vessel, *Lady Michelle*, in what was one of the biggest-ever cocaine busts in the Atlantic. But the Albanians who owned the cocaine are believed to have killed at least two of the British crew members, whom they suspected of helping authorities to snatch the load.

Essex armed robber Stan explained: 'Those two fellas just disappeared. No one knows what happened to them, but it seems they broke the rules and paid for it with their lives.

'There are certain regulations when you smuggle drugs for foreign gangs. The main one is that if your product goes missing or is snatched by the police then you are responsible for reimbursing the gangsters who hired you in the first place.

'I've known many British and foreign gangsters who "lost" drugs like this and most of them have ended up dead cos that's the rules of this game. If you can't handle it then don't go near it is what we all say and it's true.'

* * *

As already mentioned in this book, the majority of old-school British criminals ditched armed robbery years ago for what they perceived to be the less risky and more lucrative drug trade. This has made it doubly hard for British criminals to accept that foreign gangs in the UK are now carrying out the same sort of armed robberies they themselves were once famous for doing. But it is a fact that armed robberies in the UK are increasing month on month and the police have no doubt that the foreign gangs are organising and pulling off these often violent crimes.

Old-school Kent criminal Jimmy says he and his old associates have been 'left in no man's land' as a result. He explained: 'These foreigners are carrying out the sort of armed blaggings in broad daylight that we used to do thirty years ago. They don't seem to care about the risks but, today, you've got DNA, CCTV cameras, the lot.'

British criminals like Jimmy believe the mainly Eastern European gangs behind the UK's new robbery epidemic are also yet again sending out a message to their local rivals: 'They're telling us they can do what the fuck they want and we can't do a fuckin' thing about it. They're fuckin' crazy but they are making a lot more money than us, so they must be doing something right.'

A typical robbery occurred in 2018 in the town of Coleshill, in the Midlands, when armed thugs, believed to be foreign gangsters, wielding a sledgehammer held up a building society in a terrifying heist.

The two masked raiders wore black and fled from the Coventry Building Society with cash as security staff topped up an ATM machine. Workers at the bank were said to have been left 'shaken and scared'. The raiders escaped in a car; no one was injured.

The same building society was targeted a few months later when four men carrying crowbars approached two guards as they delivered cash boxes from a security van at the bank. They took three cash boxes believed to contain several thousand pounds before escaping on foot.

* * *

There is also clear evidence that the influx of foreign gangsters into the UK has led to a sharp increase in bribery and corruption inside Britain's law enforcement agencies.

In November 2018, border officer Simon Pellett, thirty-seven, was convicted over a plot to smuggle contraband into the UK. Pellett had been caught trying to bring in eight pistols, two revolvers and ammunition into the country, as well as £3.8 million worth of drugs.

As one recently retired Kent police detective said: 'The foreign gangs believe that they can bribe anyone they want. I was even offered a huge bribe by one Albanian gangster I arrested a couple of years ago. He thought it was completely normal to do that sort of thing.'

In the summer of 2018, police stumbled on a ring of Eastern European interpreters based in London who regularly worked for the police, translating for arrested prisoners. It later emerged that many of the interpreters were on the payroll of the Eastern European gangs, who used them to 'monitor' their associates after they had been arrested.

Meanwhile, foreign gangs are using boats and trucks to also smuggle cheap tax-free cigarettes from Spain into the UK, where they usually end up being sold on big housing estates and working-class areas through the country.

'The ciggie runs used to be ours,' explained former criminal Jimmy. 'Me and a couple of other Kent gangs used to own that territory and it made us millions. Then the foreigners came in and pushed us out of the way by shoving a lot of guns up our noses like they did with everything else. We tried to fight back at first, but they had many more shooters and a lot more manpower, so we backed off in the end.'

Each of the foreign gangs 'working' in the area around The Crossing has its own special 'stashes holes', where they often store guns and ammunition for months at a time.

'Only two or three people in one gang know where guns are,' explained Albanian drug lord Bari. 'That way no one tells other people and guns will stay safe.

'Sometimes guns are too "hot" to keep in stash or hand back to [the] dealer we bought from. Those have to be completely destroyed so they never connect to any gangsters or crimes.'

* * *

Despite all this, some British gangsters in the areas near The Crossing do occasionally try to fight back against the invasion of foreign gangsters.

In 2017, a gang of old-school villains raided a cannabis farm in the middle of Kent in a deliberate attempt to take over the business from a gang of Romanian growers. Former armed robber Terry takes up the story: 'These British lads had decided enough was enough and they went in very hard and fast late one night. They wanted the business for themselves and decided to just take it, just like the Eastern Europeans had done to them.

'Well, what a mistake that turned out to be! The Romanians had booby-trapped the cannabis farm and the English lads were ducking explosives going off in all directions.'

The British gangsters only survived because the police and other emergency services arrived so quickly on the scene that the furious Romanians were not able to shoot them.

Two local criminals were taken to hospital for treatment following the raid on the cannabis farm: 'They looked like they'd been in a fuckin' war zone,' said Terry.

Today, the same cannabis farm is booby-trapped with even more explosives to stop the old school British gangsters from raiding the premises ever again.

Terry explained: 'The Albanians say that if any of the Brits get blown up after breaking in here again, then they're going to take their bodies and dump them on the doorsteps of the old-school crims who live in these parts.'

These sort of skirmishes between foreign and local gangsters continue to flare up but, at the time of writing, it was still clear that the 'new kids on the bloc' were coming out on top each time. Many believe it is the vast range of criminal activities that has especially helped the Eastern European gangs to thrive.

Former bank robber Ned explained: 'The foreign gangs are like workaholics compared to us. They're into everything, even passport scams. I know one Nigerian gang who went into partnership with a bunch of Bulgarians and they were producing one hundred fake passports every week for months and months.'

Many Eastern European gangs even insist on putting tracking devices on their own cars to allay any suspicions about double-dealing amongst their own 'troops'.

Ned added: 'That's really clever because it cuts out all the paranoia which often ends in bloodshed. They can prove to each other they are not being disloyal.'

It's also claimed that many of the brothels fronted by Eastern Europeans in Britain's biggest cities even contain special rooms equipped with secret cameras for 'blackmailing purposes'.

Bari explained: 'We use blackmail many times. Sometimes it is necessary to stop important people as well as other criminals from hurting us.'

* * *

Many of the Eastern European criminals based in the UK I've interviewed for this book say that you can tell the history of a foreign gang member by the tattoos on his arms.

'If they have tattoos that are hidden so you cannot see them, then they not important,' recently retired Eastern European gangster Loli told me. He claims to be one of the lucky ones, who managed at the age of fifty-five to get out of the underworld without retribution from his bosses. 'But if tattoos are exposed on bare arm or back of neck, then make sure you study them carefully.'

Many gangsters themselves have special tattoos that mark them out as members of specific clans: 'But this can be a problem if they get sent to jail and find themselves sharing a cell with a rival clan member,' explained Loli. 'Other tattoos have religious signs because most Eastern European gangsters Catholic or Muslim. Strange bedfellows, eh?

'They also often have tattoos that feature skulls because most criminals from these places do not expect to live a long life, so they see themselves ending up as skeletons who will haunt their enemies, even after their own deaths.'

But tattoos themselves are the least of the worries for UK law enforcement. They are being stretched to breaking point when it comes to trying to monitor the tens of thousands of foreign gangsters now in the country.

8
EARS ON TARGET

Watching shipping containers being carefully lifted by a giant crane off a vast ship in Tilbury docks close to The Crossing is just part of a day's work for many criminals operating in this area.

Authorities at Tilbury try their hardest to stem the tide of contraband inside those containers, but no one can deny the sheer scale of the problem. Customs officials here regularly mount unannounced raids culminating in the opening of such containers. But as former armed robber Tony pointed out: 'For every five hundred containers coming in here, no more than one of them is opened by customs. We're talkin' thousands of containers every day – it's a mission impossible for the police.'

In early 2018, one relatively large load of cocaine was uncovered at Tilbury docks hidden in tinned fruit from East Africa. However, most criminals in these parts insist law enforcement got lucky that day because a bitter ex-employee of an Eastern European gang decided to 'grass them up' to the police.

'Stupid bastard!' observed Estuary born and bred Tony. 'That fella is probably feedin' the fish somewhere between here and Calais as we speak.'

Recently, British police and security services started using tracking devices attached to shipping containers. Often that doesn't work because foreign gangs employ a 'technician' who uses an electronic scanner to check for the presence of such trackers before they are even taken by crane off a ship. But the cocaine load uncovered by customs and police back during the raid of early 2018 did help convince British law enforcement on all sides to mount a surveillance operation like no other in the late summer of that year in a bid to try and stem the flow of drugs being smuggled into the UK.

It was clear to law enforcement authorities that highly sophisticated surveillance techniques would be essential if they were to successfully monitor the Eastern European gangs now running so many criminal activities in Kent, Essex and London. Unable to penetrate these organisations with their own undercover agents, law enforcement needed to get inside the gangs from a distance.

* * *

The twin prop Beechcraft swooping 20,000 feet above the Queen Elizabeth II Bridge would not have interested even the most criminally astute of drivers thundering over The Crossing. Gangsters tend to keep an eye and an ear open for helicopters as potential spy-in-the-sky police surveillance teams, so the twin propellers whirling away high above them would have meant very little. But in the late summer of 2018, UK police, British security services and the RAF joined forces to mount a surveillance operation specifically aimed at monitoring criminals from Essex, Kent and London who used The Crossing – with particular focus on the foreign gangs.

Usually, this sort of operation has its own unique operational codename but this one was so speculative, it didn't even merit a title. Law enforcement's weapon of choice for the complex assignment was a state-of-the-art Beechcraft surveillance plane worth in the region of £30 million. The Beechcraft could monitor targets from as high as 25,000 feet, if necessary. Ironically, British security services MI6 and MI5 had used the Beechcraft to monitor and then pinpoint the position of that same British crime lord (mentioned earlier in this book) the year before his death at the hands of a hitman in the summer of 2015. The man had his own connections to The Crossing through his alleged involvement in several multi-million-pound drug deals connected to Eastern European cartels.

The RAF's specially adapted Beechcraft aircraft was crammed with electronic eavesdropping and direction-finding equipment. The wingspans of these planes were six inches longer than standard Beechcraft models, thanks to the antennae built into them. Five more antennae could be lowered from the belly of the aircraft once the plane was in flight.

Aboard the planes, two operators with headphones worked at computers set up for listening once the aircraft had reached an altitude of between 20,000 and 25,000 feet. Not even cloud cover could prevent effective surveillance.

These operators-in-the-sky were also able to monitor four locations simultaneously. The Beechcraft was even capable of transmitting real-time streaming video footage of a target to fixed or vehicle-mounted ground receivers. The only essential element needed for this type of high-level surveillance was that the target left the battery in his (or her) mobile phone. The operators could lock onto it remotely – if and when required – without triggering the phone itself. This would enable them to get a fix on specific targets at all times of the day and night. It didn't matter how many mobile phones were thrown away, as long as the targets had one in their possession.

Surveillance specialists stationed at RAF Spadeadam, Cumbria, in the north of England, worked in conjunction with the RAF's 14 Squadron based at Waddington, Lincolnshire, from where the Beechcraft planes were dispatched on their spy-in-the-sky activities.

During that summer 2018 surveillance operation, the Beechcraft was so high above its targets that they would never have known they were even being 'watched'. Also, the Beechcraft had complete freedom to use all available air space while on such monitoring operations.

Foreign gangs in the UK had long since become obsessed with 'cleaning' rooms of listening devices by this time. At some important meetings, criminals began passing written notes to each other to avoid using their voices just in case they were being listened to by either law enforcement or their underworld rivals. But that was pretty much a pointless exercise when this kind of high-tech surveillance was being activated from planes tens of thousands of feet up in the sky.

One summer's evening, in 2018, the Beechcraft's two technicians eventually locked onto a red Ferrari heading south over The Crossing's Queen Elizabeth II Bridge. It was driving at high speed, weaving in and out of traffic as it overtook everything while travelling over the bridge before heading south towards the flatlands of Kent on the other side and the channel ports off in the distance. The car's number plates were genuine but police believed the driver was a big name in one of the UK's most powerful Albanian drug cartels.

In the control room close to The Crossing's toll booths, police officers took over the shadowing operation from the Beechcraft high above them as the aircraft veered off back to base, one hundred miles north of London. Less than two miles beyond The Crossing, a team of three unmarked police cars set off behind the Ferrari as it headed through the epicentre of the most criminally active county in the entire British Isles.

Less than thirty minutes later, the Ferrari pulled up in the car park of a service area on the M20 motorway, which connected The Crossing with the Channel ports of Dover and Folkestone. The driver of the Ferrari got out without a second glance and headed towards the shopping area. Three minutes later, another man approached the Ferrari, unlocked the door and got in. He then expertly and unhesitatingly fired up the engine and drove back onto the motorway before taking the next exit and doubling back on himself to then drive north back towards The Crossing.

Back in the lorry park on the other side of the service station, the original Ferrari driver leapt up into the cab of a British registered articulated truck and started the engine. He then moved forward as confidently as the man who had just driven off in his Ferrari.

As the huge vehicle encircled the lorry park, a BMW pulled out behind it, followed by a Skoda Estate. At the front of the lorry another BMW appeared coming towards it from the opposite direction. Then a silver Volvo estate swung out of a parking spot and moved alongside the lorry. The man in the cab smiled to himself, stopped the lorry with a blast of air from the brakes and switched off the engine.

That afternoon, the police failed to find anything illegal on board the lorry and later concluded the Albanians had most likely been testing the police surveillance system.

'The Albanians don't miss a trick,' said one Kent police officer. 'That was what we call a dry run and it must have told them we have spies in the sky, as well as all our officers on the ground. I just hope it didn't make them any more careful than they already were.'

As the police themselves so often point out, for every drugs bust of a lorry, there are at least fifty that still get through.

* * *

UK customs officials continue to closely examine many foreign gangs' numerous money transactions. In 2018, detectives uncovered bank accounts everywhere from Gibraltar to the Cayman Islands and it was clear much of it came from money laundering dirty cash earned from a wide range of nefarious activities.

These were law enforcement techniques all very similar to those used by the Drug Enforcement Administration (DEA) in America to hunt down Pablo Escobar, back in the early 1990s.

As thousands of vehicles pass through the toll gates on the south side of The Crossing every hour, police monitoring officers sit in a surveillance booth watching the traffic as it speeds through. Next to the toll gates members of another police specialist surveillance squad sit in unmarked cars, discreetly watching and analysing the vehicles automatically photographed as they enter and leave The Crossing.

One of UK Customs' most senior drugs investigators later explained: 'We were working hard on the foreign gangs, in particular in the summer of 2018, because they were master-minding huge drug and money transactions all over the world.

'We could see what was happening, but until we had some concrete evidence it was difficult to even contemplate any arrests. You can't nick someone for guilt by association.'

Despite all their efforts to maintain a low profile, the foreign gangs could no longer avoid being the subject of intense surveillance operations by British law enforcement. Further flights by Beechcraft spy planes looped over Kent and Essex at least once a week during the rest of the summer of 2018, while monitoring the movements of dozens of crimi-nals connected by The Crossing. On the ground, two-man car teams of detectives shadowed many of the recognised foreign criminals and their family members. And in the midst of all this a number of British criminals broke their own golden rule and started to come forward to help police nail the foreign gangsters once and for all because they were sick of their double-dealing games.

'I never thought the day would come when we'd rat out other criminals but the foreign gangs had driven us to do this because we was desperate,' explained former bank robber Greg.

But the British mobsters themselves had no idea of the sophisticated level of surveillance being carried out by UK's law enforcement agencies that summer.

'Back in the day, surveillance meant having a couple of cozzers sitting at the end of yer driveway in a Ford Cortina,' explained Greg. 'But times had obviously changed.'

As Albanian drug lord Bari later told me with a shrug of the shoulder: 'When police come after you like that then you can do nothing but hope they get bored eventually. But there is no way to avoid it.

'We are businessmen who have to go out and hold meetings. We have things to do. We can't stay trapped in homes, day and night, otherwise we not able to earn money.'

* * *

During one Home Counties court case in 2018, it emerged that a courier for one of the Albanians' top drug bosses was watched by police as he made weekly trips to a lay-by in Maidstone, Kent, near The Crossing, where he would meet a lorry carrying imported cocaine from the Continent.

There is no doubt that weekly consignments of cocaine like this continue to arrive in south-eastern Europe and are then moved on to the UK. The courier in this case was eventually caught when he used a fake passport on the border of two non-European countries and he was extradited to Britain.

Today, there is clear evidence that increasing quantities of cocaine brought here by foreign gangs are then being turned into crack cocaine. It is more addictive and much more lucrative for the drugs gangs because the profit margins are far bigger.

The collateral damage inflicted by this foreign crime wave is far-reaching. It can even be traced back to feuds that are still ongoing, back in the Balkans and beyond, where Eastern European crime kingpins often settle business rivalries with chilling actions.

In 2017, in one town in Albania, gangsters dressed as policemen sprayed a bar ironically called 'Living' with gunfire, killing three and wounding seven. The bar was located close to where dozens of wealthy Albanian criminals own expensive detached homes.

Not long after this, the brother of one UK-based Albanian drug lord was arrested for blowing up an opponent in another city in Albania.

'Life is cheap out there and police not so efficient as in the UK,' explained drug lord Bari. 'So sometimes it makes sense to settle feuds back home, where you less likely to get caught.'

* * *

An innate fear of foreign 'interference' in the UK underworld is said to have driven the elderly masterminds of 2015's now notorious multi-million-pound Hatton Garden robbery to recruit only old-school local 'English' criminals for their gang.

These old-timers clearly had a huge bee in their bonnets about the foreign villains who were by then ruling the south-east of England. The Brit gangsters considered them to be 'psycho bunnies', intent on murder and mayhem. They knew The Crossing had provided a transport hub for killers, kidnappers, drug smugglers and people traffickers going backwards and forwards across the English Channel via Dover and Folkestone.

Hatton Garden's so-called mastermind Brian Reader, aged seventy-two, and his elderly fellow gang members had witnessed these cold-blooded foreign criminals swaggering through their home territories over the past ten years. One gang of Albanian burglars had even outraged Reader and his friends by raiding the known homes of a number of Essex and Kent criminals and stealing hundreds of thousands of pounds worth of goods.

'They just kept taking the piss,' explained ex-robber Billy, who knew all the Hatton Garden raiders. 'Those bastards were using the Dartford Crossing to let us know they knew where some of us lived.'

Another Albanian gang – dubbed by the tabloids as 'modern-day highwaymen' – even posed as police officers and cruised the M20 and A20 in Kent, looking for cars with foreign visitors, before forcing them to stop and robbing them of all their valuables.

Billy explained: 'One of my oldest mates sat down with one Eastern European gangster at this time to try and work out yet another peace deal. This bloke pulled out a shooter and told my pal that his wife and kids would be killed if he didn't step away from his territory. *His* territory? We're talkin' about part of South-East London here. It was outrageous, a bloody liberty!'

One Kent police officer, now retired, told me: 'It must have been hard for old villains like Brian Reader and his fellow Hatton Garden robbers. Once they'd been the kings of the castle, virtually untouchable and getting on with committing their crimes in a professional and efficient manner. Then along came the foreign boys, waving guns around and telling the old British boys to get the hell away from their territory.'

But not even this so-called 'foreign invasion' could stop Reader and his gang from carrying out the Hatton Garden Job. The heist over the Easter weekend of 2015 ended up capturing the British public's imagination more than any crime since the Great Train Robbery.

Initially, the gang got away with tens of millions of pounds worth of valuables grabbed from secret safety deposit boxes in a vault beneath a shop in London's Hatton Garden, one of the world's most famous gold and jewellery districts. But within weeks of the raid, the gang were rounded up by police and six of the accused were eventually found guilty, receiving sentences of between six and seven years at their trials in 2016. Two subsequently died in prison from natural causes. Due to their old age, others will be lucky to live long enough to be released.

Today, other old-time robbers from Kent, Essex and South London believe the Hatton Garden gang might have succeeded, had they had some foreign criminals in their team.

Bank robber Reggie, from South London, explained: 'Brian Reader and his gang got caught because they didn't appreciate new technology. CCTV cameras, search records on computers, stuff like that … I hate to admit it, but the Brits have been left behind by this sort of stuff. The Eastern Europeans, on the other hand, know all about it and it's probably best to involve them in any major crimes in the UK these days, otherwise you really will end up dead or in prison.'

* * *

The invasion of Kent and Essex by foreign gangs has also caused some other types of 'collateral damage'. In 2018, an Albanian drug baron living near The Crossing found that his teenage daughter was hooked on cocaine.

Albanian drug lord Bari explained: 'Fathers are very strict with their daughters where we come from and this guy went crazy with anger when his daughter got hooked on coke. In the end, he had to have her kidnapped by his men from a drug den near The Crossing. She was taken back to Albania to "dry out". She eventually made a full recovery and took up horse riding to replace her craving for drugs. Her father was so proud that he brought his daughter back to Kent and took over riding stables by intimidating owner who owed him money. Then this poor kid had a riding accident and broke her hip. She is now permanently disabled. The man returned with his family back to Albania, saying he never wanted to work in UK ever again.'

* * *

In Central London – less than thirty miles north-west of The Crossing – some of the most blatant, outrageous examples of collateral damage caused by the foreign crime invasion can be found.

A series of deaths over a chilling four-year period in London was blamed entirely on the all-powerful St Peterburg Russian Mafia cartel alleged to have connections with Russian President Vladimir Putin.

The first death occurred in London's exclusive Sloane Square in the winter of 2010 when a lawyer for a money laundering cartel working for some of the city's wealthiest criminals and oligarchs – as well as Putin – jumped into the path of an oncoming tube train.

According to police, passengers on the platform noticed a short man in a hooded jacket standing very close to the victim just before he 'jumped'. One source from inside the money laundering cartel told me that the victim was considered a 'security risk' and had to be eliminated. His death was perceived as a suicide by British police but Russian Mafia sources say this is a classic murder method for them.

'Making it look like a suicide is the Russian Mafia's calling card,' said former London money launderer Mike. 'They want the victim's family to realise that the death was the fault of the victim, not the perpetrators. There is a strange twisted logic to it.'

Rumours then circulated London that one of the victim's friends had been talking openly about how he believed his friend was murdered by Russian gangsters and that he had been in contact with the American Drug Enforcement Agency and UK law enforcement agents.

Just before Christmas 2012, that same man died in chillingly similar circumstances as his friend when he 'fell' under a train at London's Marylebone tube station. Once again, a short man in a hooded jacket was seen close by, moments before this latest victim died. In London's money laundering circles – dominated by foreign criminals – many were saying that more people would soon be killed because they were security risks to the Russian Mafia and their oligarch clients.

Then, in November 2014, another 'property developer' with alleged connections to the same money laundering syndicate jumped to his death from the roof-top car park at Whiteleys Shopping Centre, in Bayswater, Central London.

But these so-called 'mystery deaths' weren't over yet.

Less than a month later – on 8 December 2014 – in Mayfair, Central London, another suspected millionaire money launderer 'fell' to his death from the balcony of a £5 million apartment. He was grotesquely impaled on wrought-iron railings one hundred feet below.

Many members of London's elite money laundering underworld were shaken by the series of deaths. As one criminal told me: 'I was stunned – these guys weren't even the big fish. But I heard the Russian Mafia were told to protect their clients at all costs there was any danger they might be exposed to the British government.'

Back at The Crossing, the deaths of all these men didn't merit much of a mention amongst the Eastern European gangsters running all the drugs in from Europe.

Albanian drug lord Bari explained: 'Russians kill everyone, they psychos. We just keep away from them. They do their money laundering, we do our other stuff. We're just hardworking criminals. We are not like the Russians, who shoot and then ask questions later.'

* * *

In the areas close to The Crossing, foreign gangsters remain obsessively keen to ensure that as few petty crimes as possible are committed on their hard-won territory. As drug lord Bari explained: 'We not want police sticking noses in our business round here, we just want to get on and earn our money. So, smalltime crime around these parts is bad news for us because it attracts attention.

'One gang of local kids set up a team of street drug dealers round here, few months back. That was big problem for us because police start monitoring all cars and trucks coming in and out of our area. In the end we found those kids and forced them to close down operation. One of them tried to stand up to us to impress his friends. He got two broken legs and the others left the area immediately.'

These skirmishes between foreign gangsters and local British criminals in Kent and Essex may not be apparent to most 'normal law-abiding citizens' travelling back and forth using The Crossing, but rest assured it is happening right under their noses.

The majority of Eastern European gangsters I interviewed for this book insisted pockets of trouble still flare up from time to time. As a result, foreign gangs continue to bring in 'specialists' to help sort out their feuds with the remnants of the old school British gangsters who once ruled this area.

Old-school gangster Gary told me: 'This is our fault. We should have seen those fuckin' bastards off years ago or pulled out completely then none of these problems would be happening now. But they are much harder bastards than us. They don't seem to care about innocent victims, we are just a means to an end to them. It's dangerous and it's chaos and we'll never win it back again. What a fuckin' mess!'

UK-based Czech criminal Petr summed up the attitude of these foreign 'guvnors' of The Crossing when he told me: 'We don't like having these clashes but it seems hard for the English gangsters to accept we are here to stay so we bring in other criminals from our home countries to send them a message if they cause us trouble.'

He then described how his gang 'imported' a specialist contract killer in 2018 to murder two criminal rivals they had clashed with: 'You'll never read about this because the victims just disappeared. We don't want bodies to be discovered – their associates know what happened and that is enough for us.

'Look, it was a last resort for us, but we had to stamp our authority on our enemies somehow. By using someone from outside the UK, it is impossible for our enemies to know who is actually behind the killings. That cuts down the chance of any reprisals.'

Petr refused to confirm or deny if those 'two enemies' were British or foreign.

* * *

Meanwhile, London's police forces continue to regularly try to monitor Albanian Mafia members flooding the capital's streets with cocaine. London's Metropolitan Police service has combined forces with the National Crime Agency to target such gangs.

As retired Scotland Yard drug squad detective Bert explained: 'We identify many of the Albanians through their movements back and forth across The Crossing and through the Channel ports, so we know who many of them are but that doesn't make it any easier to bring them to justice.'

In recent years, the police have particularly focused on more than 200 Albanian criminals operating on UK soil. The difficulty is that many of these syndicates are controlled by bosses based back in Eastern Europe, who never actually work on British soil.

'Those bosses pull the triggers from the safety of their own homes and don't get their fingers dirty,' said old-school gangster Ned. 'That seems to make them even more cold-blooded.'

The UK police's attempts to bring the Albanian gangs to justice remain a painfully slow process. Over the past ten years, just 130 Albanians have been successfully prosecuted in UK courts. Millions of pounds worth of drugs and cash have been seized, but this is no more than a drop in the ocean compared to the quantity of drugs successfully smuggled into this country every month. Meanwhile, the Eastern Europeans constantly evolve new and complex ways to hide cocaine in compartments built into containers, cars and trucks.

In October 2018, Latvian drug smuggler Henri Kampana was jailed for ten years after £1.4 million worth of cocaine was found in a specially constructed fuel tank on his minibus. But his arrest had nothing to do with undercover agents and two-timing criminal informants.

A sharp-eyed Border Force official at Dover's Eastern Docks actually spotted some unusual bolts keeping Kampana's minibus petrol tank in place during a routine inspection. The tank was removed and officers discovered it contained specially constructed compartments, where fourteen kilos of cocaine, each in one-kilo taped packages, were stashed.

Kampana, thirty-nine, from the Latvian region of Iecava – was later found guilty at Canterbury Crown Court after a four-day trial. The judge, Recorder Stuart Trimmer QC, said the operation was 'sophisticated' and the tank was 'a remarkable piece of work'.

Britain's National Crime Agency tried to probe Kampana for information about the gangsters who had paid him to smuggle the drugs but he refused to help them, knowing full well he would be killed if he became a police informer.

Kampana always denied knowing the drugs were in his fuel tank. He said he'd been approached by the owner of the van, who asked him if he could drive it from Iecava to London to deliver some post.

On another occasion, Scotland Yard worked with four different police forces in a surveillance and undercover operation to track one Albanian gangster. They eventually seized more than £500,000 in cash and recovered cocaine from numerous vehicles. This included £4 million worth of drugs found in one car stopped by police on Battersea Bridge, South-West London.

In another police operation, officers from Scotland Yard's Organised Crime Group seized more than 200 kilos of high-grade cocaine and arrested 20 couriers and 'trusted lieutenants' associated with another Albanian drug lord as they attempted to dismantle his network from 'bottom to top'. However, such networks are usually then reassembled and up and running again within weeks, if not days, because of the structure of the Eastern European drug gangs now based in the UK.

Foreign gangsters are also always on the lookout for new territories and vulnerable locations for their smuggling operations. As a result, these gangs have been spreading their net much further afield geographically when it comes to smuggling a wide range of their contraband into the UK. Recently, Eastern European gangs began targeting isolated coastlines in Suffolk and Norfolk, which are 'wide open' to smugglers. Law enforcement agencies have even conceded that they are often too undermanned to fully protect such remote harbours, estuaries and marinas from criminal gangs.

The rescue of migrants from the English Channel at a small Norfolk port called Sea Palling in 2018 exposed weaknesses in the UK's borders, particularly along more isolated stretches of coastline.

In early 2019, Coastwatch volunteers in nearby Pakefield – just inside the Suffolk county border – said they were the only teams keeping a regular eye on the fifty-mile stretch of coastline between their station and Felixstowe in the south.

Suffolk Police and Crime Commissioner Tim Passmore even admitted the county was 'wide open' to foreign criminals and called for defences to be tightened urgently in a bid to prevent these gangs trying to control the area.

'I think the coast here in Suffolk is particularly vulnerable,' explained Mr Passmore. 'We have thirty-one ports and marinas and it's all too easy for organised crime groups to practise their ill-gotten deeds here.

'It's not just illegal immigrants – it's arms, drugs and potentially terrorists, too.'

In April 2019, more than a dozen handguns, ammunition and twenty-nine stun guns were seized in a police operation that led to the arrest of a Latvian national in King's Lynn, Norfolk. It is believed that those arms were most likely smuggled into the UK via a nearby deserted cove.

A report from the Independent Chief Inspector of Borders and Immigration published in January 2019 also found the Border Force's knowledge of maritime threats was 'generally poor and needed to be improved'. It was even admitted in a secret NCA briefing document that foreign criminals were targeting smaller ports further up the east coast of England. With just three Border Force cutters patrolling 11,000 miles of UK coastline at any one time, senior UK security officials openly admitted the nation's maritime defences were completely over-stretched.

New powers targeting smugglers came into force in 2018 – just days after details of extra investment in strengthening border security were announced. Border Force officers can now legally stop, board, divert and detain vessels and arrest anyone they suspect of breaking immigration law. Extra patrol vessels are also set to be introduced, helping to intercept attempts to smuggle dangerous weapons, drugs and migrants into the country. The Home Office said the first vessels will be in place 'in the coming months', adding to the protection already offered by the Border Force cutters and Royal Navy vessels. Three 'maritime coordination hubs' will also be created to tackle coastal threats by building greater partnership between law enforcement and maritime partners, improving intelligence and creating a more flexible response team. But at the time of writing there was no sign of these new measures ever materialising.

* * *

In 2016 – just south of London – Albanian criminals joined forces with members of the Chinese triads to create a lucrative money laundering syndicate in order to clean the hundreds of millions being earned from a variety of criminal enterprises operated in and around The Crossing in Kent and Essex.

Fen Chen, thirty-two, was arrested by NCA officers shortly after she accepted a bag containing more than £300,000 from an Albanian called Fation Koka, thirty, in the car park of an Asda supermarket in Park Royal, North-West London.

Police also found £180,000 cash in bags and hiding places at Chen's flat, as well as a cash counting machine. Text messages were also found on phones which referred to other cash handovers.

Chen, her friend Ying Lin, twenty-seven, and two unknown associates had taken other bundles of bank notes into dozens of London banks, amounting to £2.8 million over the previous month. Another £180,000 in cash was discovered by police in bags and hiding places at Chen's London flat, along with bank slips detailing hundreds of deposits totalling a further £1.8 million.

She was eventually sentenced to six years and three months imprisonment and ordered to hand over £317,487 to authorities.

Koka was jailed for twenty-one months and ordered to be deported after completion of his sentence. Lin was deported back to China after serving a fourteen-month sentence.

Albanian drug lord Bari explained: 'Another money laundering syndicate was up and running within days of arrest. We have systems in place that allow for these problems, so we never lose business.'

Tens of millions of pounds taken off the streets by police and it still made no dent in the foreign gangs' criminal activities.

9

SWIMMING IN CASH

The back doors to a vast rusting shipping container – the Eastern Europeans' favourite mode of transport for just about everything – swung open to reveal three men pushing wads of cash into the cavity between two outside walls. It was a bitterly cold January day in 2019.

My host was an Albanian called Ruk known as 'The Collector' – 'kolektorit' in Albanian – and we were next to a shipping container close to The Crossing. Nearby was the container where I had earlier seen car registration plates changed as quickly as if they were tyres being swapped in a high-speed Grand Prix pitstop.

The Collector's job was pretty self-evident from his name. He visited all his gang's premises across areas close to The Crossing to collect the mountains of cash being earned from the Albanians' multi-layered criminal enterprises.

Another Albanian called Gerry was translating. 'Where would we be without containers?' laughed Ruk the Collector as his three men continued stuffing inch-thick bundles of twenty-pound notes frantically into the cavities between the outside and inner lining of the container. 'We always take all the cash back to Albania. Then we split it up into little bags and bring some of it back here to finance all our businesses.'

I asked why they didn't simply do all that here and avoid the risk of being stopped at customs.

'When we leave this country, no one cares. The customs men smile and wave at us because they are so happy to see us going. That's why it's so easy to take stuff out. At our own border, we bribe the guards so that's no problem either. But the main reason we store all the cash in Albania is because there are so many gangs of other foreigners and British who would come and kill us for our money if they thought we had it stashed somewhere here.'

The way the Albanians handled their cash earned from crime in the UK made complete sense. Ruk even tried to convince me it made things safer for the police and other British criminals as well.

'This way, no one gets hurt because our greedy enemies don't bother trying to find our money,' he explained.

But surely, I asked, other criminals must still be tempted to hijack the lorry carrying the container they are sending back home?

Ruk smiled.

'No one – not even these guys – knows which lorry will have this container on board,' he explained. 'Usually, we drive this one to a place in the countryside near here, where there are five other containers all the same colour. Then we change the trucks so that not even our own men know which one has the actual money in it.

'It's like those guys who point their guns in a firing squad and don't know which guns have the bullets in them. It's clever, isn't it?

'As I said, they know we take it all back to Albania so there is no point in them coming to kill us. You understand?'

After sealing the inner lining of the walls inside the container, the same men began loading assorted pieces of furniture into the same container. The armchairs and sofas appeared to be brand new and some of them were unusually shaped.

'They're all made from cartoons of money,' Ruk explained after he saw the quizzical look on my face. 'I got the idea when I was working in Spain alongside British criminals out there. They used to smuggle cheap cigarettes back here all the time by turning the cartons into armchairs and sofas and stuff like that.'

Even the 'creative' ideas for specific criminal enterprises had been mercilessly stolen from the fast-retreating British criminals by the Eastern European gangs.

* * *

Forty-five minutes later, I was sitting at a table watching Ruk swim up and down a thirty-metre pool located in the outhouse of the grounds of an isolated country house in rural Kent. On the table was Ruk's solid gold knuckleduster, which he had taken menacingly out of the pocket of his jacket before changing into his swimsuit a few minutes earlier. That knuckleduster was like a throwback to a bygone era of criminality. It even had an eagle emblem on it, which I later discovered was the motif of the Albanian gang he belonged to.

The Albanians like to say that they believe every weapon they carry is there for a purpose.

'You never know who might turn up and try to steal from us,' said Ruk a few minutes earlier when he saw me examining the knuckleduster. 'We must be armed at all times. Obviously, we don't want to use our weapons but we will not hesitate if anyone threatens us.'

Over in Albania there are numerous examples of how Britain's lucrative crimelands have economically benefited the country. On the outskirts of the capital Tirana in recent years new suburbs have been built which are lined with expensive detached houses, many of them owned by gangsters 'working' in Britain and Europe.

One veteran Albanian gangster I met called Cenki – he claimed to be the only openly gay Albanian gangster in the UK – told me that he intended to quit the UK underworld within the next year to move back home, where he would be swimming in cash for the rest of his life.

He explained: 'You'd think I'd want to stay here because they are nicer to people like me in the UK. But I like to think that with all the money I have, I will be able to look after my family without people hating my guts like they used to before I moved to the UK ten years ago.

'Sure, I have enemies because I'm gay but those guys are stupid and old fashioned. The big bosses here and back in Albania don't care if I am gay or straight, as long as I earn them much money.'

Cenki actually believes that other gangsters – both foreign and British – have underestimated his business acumen because he is gay: 'That has been to my advantage. In any case, I don't put on a show of being gay – I just get on with my job.

'My personal life is as settled as any straight person I know. I have a boyfriend in the UK and another in Albania, just like many of the gangsters have a wife here and another one back home.'

When I met Cenki he was about to leave for Albania. His means of transport for the trip across Kent, the Channel and then through much of Europe was a nondescript ten-year-old VW Passat Estate.

Cenki explained: 'Eastern Europeans love these Passats because they don't get noticed. They're the perfect car to get to places without being bothered by the cops.'
He then patted the top pocket of his jacket, pulled out a sachet and rubbed a pinch of cocaine on his gums before offering me some, which I refused.

'It's good to be alert on a long journey,' he insisted.

It was one in the morning and The Crossing was relatively quiet as Cenki drove off under the shadows of the huge girders of the Queen Elizabeth II Bridge. He then slipped onto the motorway above, which would take him through Kent and down to the Channel ports.

Less than an hour later, Cenki would pass through the customs area of Dover port. 'Don't worry, I use my real passport when I go home,' he told me before he left. 'I have nothing to hide and it's good for them to see me go home.'

Cenki's 1,500-mile journey that day would take him through France, Belgium, Germany, Austria, Croatia, Serbia, Bulgaria and finally into Albania. No doubt he'd be dipping in and out of that sachet of cocaine in order to complete the trip virtually nonstop in just twenty-four hours.

Back near The Crossing, Ruk The Collector told me that often the Albanian criminals bet money on how long it will take to complete the long drive home.

'The record is twenty hours and fifteen minutes. Not bad, eh? I know because I did it in that time and won £10,000,' he explained.

Ruk the Collector and other Albanian criminals working in and around The Crossing told me that at least one shipping container stuffed with cash was dispatched to Albania every month, usually laden with tens of millions of pounds.

Drug lord Bari explained: 'No one cares if you deal in cash for everything back in Albania. This money is good for our country. We spend money on houses and cars and that also helps the economy. That is why we are never arrested there for crimes we commit outside Albania.'

On the streets of certain cities in Albania – including the capital Tirana – it is clear that the modesty shown by many Eastern European gangsters while operating in the UK is not so apparent once they reach their homelands.

Bari explained: 'It's very different once you get home. Many have relatives in police, so we not have problems with them like you do in UK. And when you rich, people respect you more in Albania, so we not afraid to show off.'

Most gangsters' houses in Albania are filled to the brim with blingy faux French Regency furniture complete with gold-trimmed televisions and windows often fitted with bullet-proof glass. Many gangsters drive expensive cars such as Bentley Turbos and live in gated communities or behind high wrought-iron railings complete with ferocious guard dogs.

Bari offered this further insight: 'We can relax and be ourselves in Albania. Most of us have families here because we don't want them to be kicked out of Britain, so it better to keep wife and children here.'

Deep in the countryside outside the Albanian capital Tirana is a private airfield said to contain more Learjets than anywhere else in Eastern Europe. It is rumoured that drug cash earned mainly in the UK paid for the entire airport to be constructed some years ago because Eastern European criminals wanted somewhere to fly in and out of without any of the usual airport restrictions and security routines.

Albanian gangster Fido told me that some of the country's politicians sometimes charter these aircraft for trips to other countries: 'I doubt they pay much because Albanian gangsters like to make sure politicians owe them big favours,' he said.

A lot of the criminals who arrive back in their Eastern European homelands after long stints in the UK often build casinos and nightclubs in order to wash the dirty cash they have made in the UK. And many – including Bari – own luxury yachts that are kept in slick marinas, usually also built with drugs cash: 'We control ports where our boats are kept, so it's no problem,' he explained.

Some Albanian drug lords even have helipads on the roofs of their mansions.

'They proud of having so much money and they want everyone else to know about it. One guy I know even built elevator with bullet-proof glass, which takes him on the roof from his bedroom at high speed,' said Bari.

But there is a twisted 'cost' for many wealthy gangsters back in their Eastern European homelands. Bari explained: 'Some criminals back home see us and think we are even richer than we are. They try to kidnap our families to force us to pay them money so we always use bodyguards in Albania – it's safer that way.'

Many Albanian gangsters still live in close-knit family clans back in their home territories. According to Bari: 'The clans stay in their own specific territory just like gangsters back in UK. But difference here is that you try to have all your family in one place. We have big, big houses that can also be used for meeting places. These homes busy all day, all night with kids, grandchildren, old parents. Everyone is there.'

Some clans send 'on-the-road' gangs to the UK to commit crimes and then immediately return to their homeland. 'These gangs good at certain type of crimes which involve escaping cops as quick as possible,' Bari explained.

These 'on-the-road' gangs often target provincial cash-points, stealing money from bank cards, and then return to their homelands virtually millionaires from just one or two weeks of 'work'.

In 2018, one such Bulgarian gang is said to have stolen more than £3 million from UK cash machines in the space of just a few days. These gangs are also skilled at producing cloned credit cards and pin numbers, which they then insert in specific cash machines to take out money.

* * *

Many Eastern European gangsters believe that the unofficial 'turf agreement' between them and Central London's mega-rich money laundering gangsters – who work through the Russian Mafia – has helped save dozens of lives.

Albanian drug lord Bari explained: 'The streets of London would have many bodies if we'd started falling out with the Russians. No, it's better we keep businesses separate from each other, then we can both carry on making much money.'

But watching all this in the spring of 2018 was a renegade gang of old-school British criminals who had decided 'enough was enough'. They knew they didn't have the fire power to take on the Eastern Europeans so they decided to target a completely different group of so-called foreign invaders in the heart of London.

Former Essex bank robber Chris explained: 'This bunch of old-school villains went after the money laundering market in London. They was sick of watching all these foreigners earning massive amounts of cash. It was bad enough being pushed out of Kent and Essex by the Eastern Europeans. But then to see those Russian money launderers earning literally billions while they struggled must have seemed totally out of order.'

In May 2018, a three-man team of Essex-based British gangsters started pitching their money laundering skills to some of London's richest residents, including a number of oligarchs and Russian 'businessmen' still living in the UK capital at that time.

The British money launderers were secretly being 'financed' by two old-school London crime families, who had decided it was time to take back what they believed rightfully belonged to them in the first place.

Chris explained: 'The British lads undercut the "interest" rate being charged by the main Russian-financed money laundering gang in London. The local criminals also made it clear there would be a war if they didn't start getting a share of the laundering business.'

Eventually, a small group of oligarchs and other wealthy 'entrepreneurs' in London agreed to try out the British launderers without telling the Russian-run gang they'd been using for many years. However, word soon got out that the Brits were stealing business from the long-established laundering gang with close connections to the Russian Mafia and Vladimir Putin.

'That's when all hell broke loose,' said Chris. 'It turned into the gunfight at the O.K. Corral. The British boys had toughened up a lot after suffering at the hands of the Eastern Europeans for so long and the Russians – well, no one fucks with them, do they?

'It got pretty messy. A couple of the Brits' soldiers went missing. Then a couple of the money laundering gang's Russian heavies disappeared. It was turning into a classic tit-for-tat massacre.'

Meanwhile, a number of London-based oligarchs became so alarmed by these new underworld battles which had erupted on their doorstep that they suddenly left the city and set up home as far afield as Israel and Spain.

'It wasn't until February of 2019 that it finally all calmed down,' explained Chris. 'But in that time, almost half the money laundering business from inside London had gone abroad because everyone was panicking. And that didn't leave much for those British lads to get their hands on.'

In the midst of all this, a number of British criminals even turned informants for the police and security services when they realised the oligarchs were leaving British shores so would not be putting any business their way.

Chris explained: 'Some of those oligarch types were so rich that their lawyers got advance notice that they were being investigated and then they simply left the UK for good. What a waste of bleedin' time! The British boys shouldn't have given up all those territories in Essex and Kent to the Eastern Europeans in the first place then none of this would have happened.'

By the middle of 2019, the atmosphere between the foreign and old-school British gangs seemed to have once more calmed down. Chris said: 'But those foreign guys are still running things and we've been left with a lot of egg on our face and not much else.'

Some old-time British gangsters are convinced that eventually they and their adult children – combined with some new London faces emerging from the underworld – will mount an offensive against all the foreign 'invaders' which will see them forever thrown off UK soil.

'But that's not going to happen overnight,' said Chris. 'For the moment the British lads are a spent force. It's sad, but it's the way the underworld round these parts has been going for a long time.'

Meanwhile, back in the areas surrounding The Crossing, the Eastern European gangs continue going from strength to strength. Romanian drug baron Tiri revealed to me that his gang had recently even begun laundering drug money through fixed-odds betting terminals in bookies across Britain.

'It's a simple process because the British love to gamble so there are thousands of outlets, which is perfect for this type of operation,' he explained.

* * *

The majority of the Eastern European gangsters I have spoken to for this book admit they deliberately avoid legal property ownership in the UK for fear that it could be confiscated if they were ever arrested. However, some foreign criminals do 'own' houses in the UK, despite their names not being on the deeds. These properties are often taken over in lieu of outstanding debts from drug deals and other criminal enterprises.

In some cases, Eastern European gangsters have used threats of violence to force UK citizens into retaining legal ownership of properties despite foreign gangsters living in those properties full time. And it's not just drugs that form the backbone to the foreign invasion of those areas close to The Crossing: stolen gold and gems also make these gangs tens of millions of pounds each year.

In recent years, yet more shipping containers have been converted into specialist 'handling centres' where stolen jewellery, gold and silver can be 'stripped down' by removing precious stones and then selling them off separately. These stones are often then smuggled to Antwerp, Belgium, where they are sold to legitimate dealers. Drug lord Bari explained: 'There is a "run" to Antwerp every single week from UK because we have so many burglary gangs bringing stuff in.'

Essex gangster Geoff admitted: 'The Eastern Europeans don't miss a trick and while we'd been obsessing about drug dealing, they've branched out in every direction including running their own teams of burglars who bring in millions of pounds' worth of valuables every month.'

* * *

By the winter of 2018, the online boasts of the Albanian Hell-banianz gang based in London were so outraging other, more traditional Albanian criminals in the UK that 'action' was taken against them.

Drug lord Bari explained: 'The Hellbanianz youngsters got too big for their boots. They thought they owned the universe because they were selling so many drugs for the Albanian Mafia. They were so out of control, they organised knife fights with other gangs in public places in London. They thought they were untouchable.

'Then they posted yet more stuff on Instagram showing lots of cash and drugs and jewellery. The rest of us were already very angry from their earlier online behaviour but now they were exposing us all and we knew police would come down on us hard if we didn't sort them out.'

So just before Christmas 2018, a team of twelve Albanians from other gangs agreed to form a unit to kidnap some of the Hellbanianz members 'to teach them a lesson'.

Bari explained: 'We wanted to maybe cut a finger or two off and then get the Hellbanianz to stop their boasting and let us all get on with our business.'

But the Hellbanianz were outraged when three of their men were snatched from the streets of London.

'They came back at us with guns blazing, literally,' said Bari. 'They should have stopped and thought about what was happening, but they take too many drugs to be able to work it out.'

At least half a dozen Albanian criminals working in the south-east of England went missing as the two warring factors clashed. Bari explained: 'Hellbanianz thought police would not care because it was Albanians hurting other Albanians. But they were wrong. Cops not like this happening here in case innocent people get hurt or killed.

'So, after a few guys went missing, we found ourselves the target of police raids, as well as exchanging fire with the Hell-banianz. It was a fuckin' nightmare!'

Eventually – just after Christmas of that year – the Hellba-nianz and at least three older Albanian clans met and agreed a peace pact amid fears that their fighting was helping to create a vacuum which old-school British criminals might try to step back into.

Bari explained: 'Luckily, British gangsters did not realise quickly enough what was happening, otherwise we'd have started losing territories.'

Kent criminal Eddy Roberts later explained: 'We only heard what was happening between the Albanians after it was all over. It was typical. None of us had our ears to the ground. If we had then maybe we'd now be back in business.'

Albanian drug lord Bari's overview sums up the state of the current so-called peace agreement between the Eastern European criminals who operate near The Crossing and the old-school British gangsters who still want their former territories back but don't have the cash, muscle or firepower to do much about it.

Bari said: 'This part of UK belongs to us now, not British gangsters. We never give this up. I hope the British criminals go away because if they do not, then they will be destroyed when we come after them again. They need to be very careful.'

*   *   *

The Crossing's foreign-registered trucks with their many shipping containers continue to carry illegal immigrants, drugs, cigarettes and sex workers as well as a vast range of old-fashioned contraband. These are the UK underworld's new bread and butter, the key ingredients that helped enable the foreign gangs to win their underworld war with their British counterparts in the first place.

Residents who live in and around the areas close to The Crossing have recently claimed there has been a sharp increase in what hardworking, ordinary citizens consider to be collateral damage since the Eastern European gangs took over the local underworld.

'There have been a lot of beatings where men turn up at houses, charge in with baseball bats and smash the living daylights out of people they think have crossed them,' said one longtime Dartford resident. 'This sort of thing never happened until the foreign gangs turned up here. Then there are all the kids hooked on drugs that are being virtually drip-fed them by the street drug dealers, most of whom are Eastern European.' And it's still rare for UK law enforcement to actually take any 'Big Fish' off the streets.

Today, the NCA has a number of officers stationed in Eastern Europe in an attempt to gather information on the crime networks who have invaded British soil. But close-knit family ties make the Mafia clans as hard as ever to penetrate and news of police presence in any town soon reaches the local gangs.

*   *   *

Meanwhile, the Eastern European gangsters operating in and around The Crossing often use 'spotters' on scooters to ensure they know if and when any police or other 'intruders' visit the dimly lit streets, warehouses and lorry parks close to the Queen Elizabeth II Bridge.

Romanian people smuggler Kilo explained: 'We use local kids sometimes or Eastern European teenagers living on nearby council estates because it's important to know what is happening on our territory.'

These 'spotters' are usually given a free Nokia 'non-smart' throwaway mobile phone and ten pounds of credit each week in exchange for calling the foreign gangsters whenever they see any unfamiliar people or vehicles in the areas around The Crossing.

And those same gangs of youths on scooters have also been used for something even more sinister.

10
THE FUTURE

You'd never know it unless you went searching for it, but often when darkness falls in the areas around The Crossing, youths in hoodies tour the streets on their scooters armed with high-powered air guns and baseball bats.

Every time they see a CCTV camera within reach they take aim with their guns or smash it with their baseball bats. Their reward from the foreign gangsters who have taken over this area in recent years is yet more free credit for their throwaway phones.

In another part of this strange netherworld is a shipping container with six men inside it systematically grinding down and then cutting and re-cutting cocaine in order to 'stretch' it out to provide the Albanians with three times more profit than if they had simply sold the cocaine straight from their South American suppliers.

The process of cutting cocaine varies across the world but an Albanian called Peta is the self-acclaimed king of cutting in these parts. Using a kitchen Magimix domestic food mixer to blend the final product and two plastic bowls, he sieves the white powder and then sprinkles whole spoonfuls of 'cutting powder' (usually baby laxative) from a plastic container into the cocaine until he believes he has achieved the 'perfect mix'. Peta and two other 'experts' then test the cocaine by snorting a long line to make sure it still delivers some kind of 'hit'.

The cocaine is then packed into £20 and £40 baggies, which are placed in plastic shopping bags to be collected by scooter boys, who arrive at the container one at a time to avoid attracting attention.

'It's like a factory conveyor belt,' said Albanian drug lord Bari. 'We are all about maximum profits and we always need to get product onto streets quickly. It doesn't earn us any money sitting around.'

The scooter boys then head out from The Crossing area to nearby towns and villages across Kent and Essex, where cocaine, hash and ecstasy are in big demand – everyone from schoolchildren to OAPs. The only clue as to what the scooter boys are up to is the distinctive shrilling sound of their machines as they arrive in each community.

Village greens and the edge of town parks are the most popular locations for the dealers on two wheels. Their customers don't wish to be under the glare of bright lights any more than they do. Each dealer takes no longer than fifteen minutes in any one spot. Then it's on to another location before anyone in authority even realises there was a drug dealer in their midst.

Some scooter dealers store at least half their product in pre-arranged stash points on the outskirts of each town they visit, just in case they do get pulled over by the police. These stash points are often under hedges or in quickly dug holes in the corner of deserted fields, close to roads.

Many of these young Eastern European scooter gangsters are encouraged by their bosses and families to prove themselves as professional criminals by working these drug 'territories' across Kent and Essex. Former Kent drug dealer Alex explained: 'I know this Romanian kid of about seventeen and he was told to go and sell some drugs in one particular town near The Crossing.

'He told me his father and grandfather back home in Romania said he needed to go out and prove himself as a criminal. Within weeks, this kid had sewn up the entire town. He had special "sales corners" where punters would meet him for drugs after texting him ahead.

'The noise of his scooter was like an alert to all the druggies in that town that their man was on the manor and packed with stuff to sell them.'

According to Alex, this same teenage Romanian drug dealer then started dating a girl who was one of his best customers. She also happened to be the daughter of an old-school British criminal, who didn't like her taking any drugs, even though he'd been known to deal in them in the past.

Alex explained: 'One day, this Romanian kid turned up dead in a ditch. No one in the town knew who he really was because he never used his real name and he didn't have any identification on him. It took three weeks before his family were even informed he was dead. When they finally got the cozzers to release the body, they gave him a proper funeral back in Romania.'

The old-school English criminal whom many believe was responsible for killing the Romanian teenager moved to Thailand with his family shortly after the murder.

'Smart move,' added Alex. 'I heard the Romanians put a hit out on that old boy but I've no idea if they ever found him.'

Politicians in Kent claim that the influx of foreign gangsters in the area has even led to the emergence of unofficial no-go areas in certain parts of the county. They have specifically named towns such as Margate, Medway and Gravesend, where they claim Eastern European street dealers are selling drugs on street corners without any apparent interference from the police.

'The reality is that the police don't have the resources to spend their entire time patrolling just one part of each community,' said one Margate resident. 'As a result, drug dealers are pretty much left alone. No wonder they're here.'

Street dealer Hari, from Bulgaria, told me that he never faced any problems with police in the Kent towns where he operated most nights of the week.

'These places are so easy to work in because there are no police around,' he explained. 'Sometimes they appear just to show the local people they are concerned but they never bother to try and arrest me or any of the other street dealers I know.'

Meanwhile, as night-time fell near The Crossing, even darker events occurred that most locals would never even have realised were happening.

* * *

The double back doors of a huge shipping container flew open and a man's body slumped to the ground. Two men stood, hands on hips, at the entrance to the opened container as two other men appeared from a nearby parked Mercedes limousine. All four of them then dragged the man's body towards the boot of the car.

Back inside the container, a woman's screams could be clearly heard until the double doors were pulled shut from the inside.

Albanian drug lord Bari takes up the story: 'He was a bad man, a Romanian truck driver who did people smuggling. He attacked one of the girls in club and when security men threw him out of container, he hit head and die.'

Bari alleged that the men running the container brothel near The Crossing dumped the Romanian's body in the nearby Thames Estuary and, in all likelihood, his corpse would have been swept by the strong current under the Queen Elizabeth II Bridge, past Tilbury and then out into the English Channel.

Bari continued his story: 'Then they stripped his truck of everything in it, including passport, and burnt it all. That truck was then resprayed and the Romanian plates replaced with Bulgarian ones. It was then sold to another haulage company.'

The way that the murdered lorry driver was dealt with is a chilling reminder to anyone who says the foreign gangs are not so bad.

As Bari admitted: 'We come from places where death no big deal. That guy had it coming, he should not have disrespected girl or men working at club.'

Not only are the foreign gangs here in the UK to stay but it seems they are not afraid to use any weapon at their disposal to ensure they remain the 'top dogs'.

* * *

So, the British gangs seem to have retreated from London, Kent and Essex for now at least. Retired criminal Ned has frequently urged his former associates to stay in the shadows if they wish to lead long and healthy lives: 'Most of us are out of our depth with these foreign gangs. We don't know how or where to hurt them and they're just poking fun at us and I don't blame them. It's time to step back completely and leave them to it.'

Other old-school gangsters remain convinced they will be able to get their old territories back one day. One told me: 'It's gonna take time and we're all gonna have to put our grievances with each other to one side and unite on all fronts. Then we have to raise the money to pay for a proper army, properly trained, prepared to do anything to force those fuckin' foreign bastards out of our country.'

Other old-time UK villains see this foreign victory as 'a sign of the times'. Ned explained: 'Computers are gonna run everything soon. Even drugs'll be downloaded from the internet one day, so you can get them in 3D or some such shit.

'Us older ones may have had it, but we owe it to our kids and grandkids to get our territories back and make a fresh start and try to return everything to the way it once was.'

Meanwhile, the Eastern Europeans' surge through Kent and Essex continues.

In 2018, one all-powerful family of Eastern European gangsters broke the 'rules' by brazenly moving onto a residential compound deep in the Kent countryside less than thirty miles drive from The Crossing.

'Families usually stay back in their homelands but this gangster wanted to be with family in UK permanently,' Bari explained. 'It's a fantastic property, very impressive and in good location, so he decided to settle here.'

This particular compound in central Kent is on the edge of a small rural community renowned for farming and little else.

Bari told me: 'I can't say where exactly it is for security reasons but I know this property was owned by very famous British criminal for many years. Then he went to prison and his wife had no choice but to sell it to Albanian crime boss because her husband owed this man much money. She continued as registered owner and Albanian boss shipped twenty closest family members and six dogs over to live in house.'

Today, the property – hidden at the end of a long driveway in the midst of thick forest – has become the headquarters of one of the most powerful Eastern European clans to have settled in this area.

Bari continued: 'This place is perfect because you get to Channel ports in thirty minutes from it. If anyone tried to spy on house then it would be obvious because it is in the middle of countryside and has many CCTV cameras in grounds.'

Those who have visited the property describe it as mock Tudor and filled with over-priced faux French furniture and lots of gaudy beige thick-pile carpet. Even the toilets have gold handles and taps, apparently.

Bari said: 'It's always full of people walking around, having meetings in different outhouses and corners of main house. And in the centre of house is this one guy, who scares so many other Eastern Europeans and British gangsters. But in this house, he is simply called "Papa" by all his family.'

According to Bari, the gang boss's teenage children are all home-taught, so they don't forget their native tongue, as well as to learn good English.

Recently, the eldest teenage daughter of the gang boss announced she was pregnant by a local man, who turned out to be the son of a well-known British criminal, who had recently died. The former gangster had been involved in several of the biggest robberies in British criminal history and – until his death two years earlier – had been at the forefront of the British underworld's once bloody war with the so-called foreign invaders.

Bari explained: 'I thought this would cause big trouble because this boy had uncles who were still trying to take back territory now belonging to this gang boss and his men. But this Albanian boss liked the boy, so he ordered his daughter to marry him. It was one hell of a wedding – Albanians at one end of marquee and British at the other! But they all behaved themselves and happy couple soon settled down. I hear boy has moved in with in-laws on compound and he is now working for father of girl.'

According to three separate sources, other Eastern European gangs are now worried that this gang boss will join forces with his new son-in-law's family and they could end up more powerful than any other Eastern European gang in the UK.

* * *

There is no doubt that many of the Eastern European gangsters flooding into the UK in recent years know exactly how to play this country's generous social services 'system' as well.

In April 2018, a Romanian gangster was free to walk the streets of Britain because 'overcrowded' jails in his homeland were judged to have breached his human rights. Convicted mobster Adrian Preda, thirty-six, had been sentenced to nine and a half years in prison in Romania for attempted murder, blackmail and organised crime. But the one-time champion cage-fighter skipped bail and went on the run, ending up in Britain. However, a judge here ruled against extraditing Preda back home in case overcrowded Romanian jails breached his right to avoid 'degrading' treatment.

Back in Romania, Preda's gang – called 'The Sportsmen' – had flooded Europe with millions of pounds worth of heroin, as well as stealing machine guns and pistols from a Romanian army base. They also frequently opened fire on rival gangsters in the streets.

Preda had even been found guilty of threatening to order the murder of a man to whom he'd given a high-interest loan, as well as sparking a turf war with a rival gang called 'The Cats'. He was just one of the latest in a string of Eastern European criminals exploiting some of the UK's numerous legal loopholes to stay in the UK by using human rights laws to prevent themselves being sent back.

In April 2019, a Turkish criminal was allowed to stay in the UK because his membership of a UK gang was deemed to be evidence he had integrated into British society.

Turkish national Tolga Binbuga, twenty-nine, had first come to the UK with his family when he was nine but he was later convicted of offences including robbery, assault and burglary. He was also linked with a notorious North London gang called 'The Get Money Gang'. But when the rest of his family were granted British citizenship in 2010, Binbuga did not even bother making an application himself.

The Home Office tried to deport Binbuga in 2014, but multiple legal appeals were then launched against this decision with a judge ruling in 2016 that he should be allowed to remain here because he could be regarded as a 'home-grown criminal'.

* * *

While there are many rumours about murders committed by foreign gangsters and their British rivals near The Crossing, not all have been fully substantiated. Some criminals even believe a lot of these stories have been deliberately spread around Kent to strike fear into the community, as well as the old-school British underworld. But there is one mass murder that I keep hearing about, which many British and foreign criminals say they know is true.

It is said that three Albanian gangsters were murdered close to The Crossing in a chilling revenge killing just before Christmas 2018. Albanian drug lord Bari explained: 'These three men were suspected of talking to police, which was pretty stupid because that type of information always gets back to gangs in the end.'

Other criminals say that all three men were rounded up from their homes on a council estate near The Crossing and shot in the head. Then their corpses were cut up and secretly fed to pigs at a 200-acre farm belonging to a member of a British crime family.

Bari said: 'I'm sure it's true because these men disappeared and have never been seen here or back in Albania since. This British gangster doesn't even know the three Albanians were killed on his land. It's a clever move because if British criminals upset foreign gang who murdered those men, then they will tell the police the bones of the three men can be found on grounds of British man's house and he'll then get arrested.'

* * *

But what does the future hold for Britain's increasingly violent crimelands? Many gangsters and police predict the body count will get much higher as the foreign gangs continue to consolidate their operations on UK soil.

Bari explained: 'Eastern European gangsters need to keep sending out messages to British that they will be wiped off face of earth if they don't stay away. So that means committing occasional murder just to remind British how dangerous we can be.'

Meanwhile, the UK has recently begun attracting criminals from countries much further afield than Eastern Europe. Refugee crises in countries such as war-ravaged Libya and numerous African countries have opened the door for many criminals to disguise themselves as homeless refugees seeking asylum in Britain.

* * *

Back on the streets of London, increasing numbers of Eastern European youths have begun to join forces with British teenage gangsters to commit muggings, robberies and sell drugs on the streets. Older Albanian criminals say this will lead to big problems.

Bari explained: 'It's not good that all these kids join up with each other in places like London, Birmingham, Manchester. It makes them too powerful, which means they are a threat to more traditional gangs. Better to keep them apart.'

The connections between these young criminal groups and the knife crime epidemic sweeping Britain have already been covered in this book. But criminals like Bari have no doubt that the knife culture in the UK will continue because it is being fuelled by the criminal enterprises he and his associates are involved with.

'The trouble is that all problems with knife crimes can only get worse as result,' he said. 'Kids think they need to carry and even use knives to control their territories. Until that changes, deaths will continue.'

* * *

And while the foreign crime epidemic in and around The Crossing continues to thrive, occasionally the police do actually manage to make their presence felt.

Take the dramatic police chase in February 2018 involving helicopters, which eventually came to an abrupt end near The Crossing.

Crews from both Kent and Surrey police forces were involved in the operation which was sparked by a theft investigation involving Eastern European gangsters. Footage shot by a Surrey police helicopter showed the chase as it came to a halt between the Swanley turn-off and Darenth Interchange in the heart of territory close to The Crossing.

* * *

In the heartlands of Kent between The Crossing and the Channel ports of Dover and Folkestone, Albanian and Romanian drugs gangs have devised a new way to smuggle contraband. Countless drugs are hidden in so-called stash houses in the middle of the county and then picked up by empty lorries that have just arrived on British soil from Europe.

Bari explained: 'It's better than bringing drugs over in one vehicle from Europe because British customs often follow trucks from Channel ports all way up to The Crossing and beyond, if they believe drugs are on board them.'

* * *

So, the Eastern European gangs continue to rake in huge amounts of cash from so-called traditional criminal activities ranging from drug dealing to prostitution. However, they still ignore many of the obvious new criminal opportunities provided by the internet.

Drug lord Bali explained: 'Criminals from Eastern Europe are very old fashioned in that way. We don't trust the internet and that has probably meant we've lost out on some good business. But we didn't want to attract attention to ourselves and I think that would have happened if we'd started committing internet crime.

'For years it seemed better to leave that sort of stuff to the Nigerians and others. They like to hide behind computer screen while committing their crimes. We've always liked to look our victims right in the eye so they know what they can expect – it's a very different mindset.'

However in recent months, the Eastern Europeans have begun to look more closely at the internet as a serious criminal enterprise. Bari explained: 'We have started to encourage younger gangsters to work outside drug business because, one day, drugs will be made legal, so we need to make our big money somewhere else.'

So, this could mark the Eastern Europeans' entry into the world of cybercrime after years of carefully avoiding it. In the long term that could mean many foreign gangsters return to their home countries, where they can easily run their internet crime operations.

'That's what you would think,' said Bari. 'But many Eastern European kids like it here and will stay, I am certain of that.

Only time will tell what will really happen, but it is important to always have one eye on future.'

Back in and around the Balkans, the few remaining gangsters who did not take part in the 'invasion' of Europe and the UK were committing some very daring crimes.

In March 2019, a gang of Albanian robbers pulled off a plane heist at the international airport in Vienna. To many, it looked like a throwback to the old days of the 1980s when Britain's professional criminals were considered masters of the art of armed robbery.

Former bank robber Steve, from Kent, said: 'I was stunned by that job in Vienna. It was beautifully executed, even though one of them did get shot dead. But, hey, that's the risk you take when you try and pull off a job like that.'

The Albanian gang who carried out the robbery were believed to have got away with £25 million, none of which has ever been recovered. Not even the death of one of their comrades quelled the admiring tone of the media coverage of this robbery.

'In their eyes losing one man was a small price to pay,' explained one seasoned foreign crime analyst. 'Those guys were highly professional and there is no doubt they will find more banks and cash warehouses to hit throughout Europe. I fully expect more of those sort of crimes to be committed over the coming years.

'The Eastern Europeans seem to see it as their right to target anything they think they can make money out of. There are no restrictions. The harder the better, as far as they are concerned.'

* * *

Today, the Eastern European gangs operating within the vicinity of The Crossing and throughout London, Essex and Kent have only a handful of old-school British criminals to contend with. But those foreign gangs continue to inform local police about the British criminal contingent.

Former Kent bank robber Kelly said: 'It's typical. This is what we have to contend with these days. We've been humiliated and they even grass us up to the police.'

Albanian drug lord Bari explained: 'We do not like informing on other gangsters, whoever they are, but doing this helps get rid of the British completely and the police give us a bit more freedom if we help them.'

In late January 2019, yet another people smuggling operation was busted near The Crossing. This time a lorry driver following behind a large articulated truck caught on video camera the moment 'illegal immigrants' jumped out of the vehicle onto the busy M25 motorway, close to the Queen Elizabeth II Bridge.

'They were lucky they didn't get run over,' one eye witness later observed.

The immigrants disappeared into a myriad of streets in nearby Dartford, Kent, and were never caught by police. Chances are they were most likely from Eastern Europe and will probably have re-joined the criminals who brought them over because their passports and cash would have been kept from them during the trip to the UK.

* * *

There are genuine fears that Eastern European drug dealers will soon start using the highly addictive opioid drug Fentanyl to help 'stretch' out their cocaine.

Old-school Kent criminal Micky Hart said: 'If those foreign lads really do start using Fentanyl, they could end up with a lot of deaths on their hands.'

It seems that nothing is off-limits when it comes to the criminal activities of Britain's new elite gangsters.

AND FINALLY....

A few days before I was due to deliver the completed manuscript of this book to my publisher, I got a call from one of gun dealer Ray's oldest friends, Keith. He was worried about former policewoman Ray, who he said was 'in deep' with a gang of Albanian drug smugglers, who had been buying guns from her frequently over the previous few months.

'They're a right evil bunch and Ray has allowed them to virtually take over her business. At first, I didn't know what'd got into her,' he explained. 'Then I heard her daughter was dating the son of one of these Albanians and they were putting Ray under pressure to organise a wedding and she wasn't so keen.

'I've heard more whispers that Ray definitely is working undercover for the police and that she had been ordered to let her daughter marry this boy because it would enable Ray to get even closer to the Eastern Europeans. If that's true, it's madness because the Albanians won't let her take another breath if they think she's working for the Feds.

'I dunno what is the truth about all this, but Ray's got to tread carefully otherwise they'll do her, I'm sure of it.'

Whatever the truth, it is highly unlikely this will be the last we will ever hear about Ray.

* * *

UK police have no doubt that the Eastern European gangsters dominating the UK's drug market now handle more than 90 per cent of all the cocaine flooding into this country.

'They have the power now,' explained one retired drugs squad officer. 'They can kill and maim people at will if anyone gets in their way. It's frightening. No wonder there is now so much fear and paranoia out there.'

Rumours of hits on innocent people and attacks on the relatives of criminals are rife in those areas of Kent, Essex and London close to The Crossing. The Eastern Europeans in particular will stop at nothing to continue to consolidate their position of power, especially in the south-east of England.

These days, the criminal badlands in and around The Crossing are now so overrun with foreign gangs that wanted British criminals have even been paying these so-called foreign invaders for protection.

In early 2019, a thirty-one-year-old runaway gangland murderer from a well-known British crime family used a Romanian drug lord's private jet to escape justice and flee to Eastern Europe. The man was later described in court as one of Britain's most-wanted murder suspects after he was alleged to have slit a twenty-one-year-old man's throat in a London bar before leaving the country.

As Albanian drug lord Bari explained: 'This case sums everything up perfectly. The British gangs have fallen apart, now they turn to us to protect them from the police. We have won!'

* * *

Professional criminal Danny, from Kent, comes from a long line of British gangsters. His father was a bank robber, his grandfather held up post office vans in the 1950s.

Danny voted for the UK to leave Europe in the 2016 EU referendum and has clearly been heavily influenced by his family's past history: 'My dad says it was all our fault the foreigners decided to take over our territories. We thought we were the kings and they'd never dare to take us on. How wrong could we be? But we're English and proud of it and it's time we took back our territories that have been stolen from us by these foreign bastards.'

Police fear that if Brexit doesn't end up changing the criminal landscape in these parts then it will lead to an even more dangerous underworld war than the one featured in this book. One retired drug squad detective told me: 'I think there'll be a bloodbath after Brexit finally goes through because all these old dinosaur local villains can't seem to get it in their thick heads that the foreign gangs are not going to just disappear. It's a powder keg scenario and there isn't much the police will be able to do to stop it.'

One former estuary criminal told this author: 'It's gonna get really nasty. The foreign gangs are settled here now and it will take another war to even start to get them out. I feel sorry for the police. With Brexit in place, they'll be expected to force the foreign criminals out of this country and those gangsters will shoot back with everything they have. I think the police will suffer heavy casualties just as the old-school villains have over the past decade.'

He added: 'And at the end of the day what will Brexit have really achieved? Fuck all.'

So there you have it; Brexit has ripped apart the criminal landscape in the UK. Leaving Europe is not the easy solution that so many nationalists predicted. And no doubt the UK underworld will emerge as an even more chilling and dangerous criminal environment once all that Brexit 'dust' has settled.

ENDNOTE

In this book I have had to protect the innocent and not so innocent by changing names and events but I have always retained
the true dramatic thread of this story. While some will no
doubt criticise me for 'helping' the guilty avoid justice, it should
be pointed out that unless this chilling underworld is exposed
– in whatever way possible – then there is no chance that law
enforcement will ever stamp it out in the near future.

For the moment, the foreign gangs who have swamped the
UK appear to be here permanently. The length of their stay in
this country will depend on people realising what they are up
to and pressurising the police and politicians to take effective
action in the long term. Therefore, I make no apology for the
style in which this book has been written as it exposes a reality
which is 100 per cent true and accurate.